'Garry is an outdoor innovator, and *The Creativity Factor* is a beautiful intersection between theory, practice and a lot of experience developed over the years. Outside thinking is powerful stuff and is now even more accessible to everyone. Enjoy this fantastic journey!'

João Perre Viana, Founder of Walking Mentorship

'Our bodies are not there just to carry our heads around. Garry Pratt makes a powerful case for utilizing the power of movement and walking for thinking and innovation. If you ever need inspiration to get out of the "bored" room to out and about, read this book and you might be walking with a new spring and purpose in your step.'

**Dr. Mia Keinänen, leadership advisor,
Russell Reynolds Associates**

'Garry successfully debunks the myth that it takes a genius or Stanford drop-out to build a successful business; we are all capable of brilliantly creative, innovative ideas. Garry's excellent insight is that we need to learn to walk with the idea.'

**Jonny Ohlson, Founder and
Executive Chair, Touchlight**

THE CREATIVITY FACTOR

Using the power of the outdoors
to spark successful innovation

GARRY PRATT

BLOOMSBURY BUSINESS
LONDON • OXFORD • NEW YORK • NEW DELHI • SYDNEY

BLOOMSBURY BUSINESS
Bloomsbury Publishing Plc
50 Bedford Square, London, WC1B 3DP, UK
29 Earlsfort Terrace, Dublin 2, Ireland

BLOOMSBURY, BLOOMSBURY BUSINESS and the Diana logo are trademarks
of Bloomsbury Publishing Plc

First published in Great Britain 2022

A catalogue record for this book is available from the British Library

Library of Congress Cataloging-in-Publication data has been applied for

ISBN: 978-1-3994-0037-4; eBook: 978-1-3994-0034-3

2 4 6 8 10 9 7 5 3 1

Typeset in Minion Pro by Deanta Global Publishing Services, Chennai, India
Printed and bound in Great Britain by CPI Group (UK) Ltd, Croydon CR0 4YY

To find out more about our authors and books visit www.bloomsbury.com and
sign up for our newsletters

For Siobhain, of course

Contents

About the author

Garry Pratt is an entrepreneur, group walking leader, reluctant academic of sorts and a recovering archaeologist. He has worked at the University of Bath in the UK as Entrepreneur in Residence and as a Teaching Fellow in Entrepreneurship, through which he has worked with the founders of over 180 early-stage tech companies. Garry says that he likes helping interesting people grow interesting businesses. He wears outdoor gear, not suits. He is a compulsive doodler. He doesn't do long meetings and believes that it is always better to walk and talk than look at a PowerPoint presentation. Although involved in high tech since the early nineties, he lives in the decidedly low-tech historical city of Bath in south-west England with his wife and three kids, dog, cat and an immortal fish. This is his first book.

Foreword

I truly believe that the future of the world will be reliant on creativity. Creativity is the life blood of the future. It is the oil for industries to come. Artificial intelligence will help with the mundane, but we will all have to be to able think outside of the box more and more to generate real innovation, and to address the big problems we collectively face.

Whether on the field of sport or in the boardroom, raw talent is important, and creative individuals are rightfully applauded, but creativity needs to be worked at, it needs nurturing, and it needs time and space to flourish. In my post-rugby career as an executive coach and entrepreneur I work with senior executives, teams and boards across multiple sectors; from finance, investment banking and commodity trading, to tech, retail and manufacturing. For me, effective coaching is underpinned by self-understanding and development of one's own performance and creativity. I appreciate deeply the correlation between sport and business and know how much can be achieved when individuals unite to strive for a common goal: self-empowerment, discipline and subscription to a winning ethos are fundamental to a culture of success in both professional domains. I often say that you've got to walk the talk before you can inspire others through your actions. I've often meant this metaphorically, but also literally, and Garry takes the literal a step further and calls on us all to actually walk ourselves creative.

Through my own business, my coaching and speaking, often considering the future of work, I come across many books that address the role of wellbeing, aim to make us happier or are focussed on success, but few strive to address all three as this book does.

Defining Garry Pratt is not easy – academic, entrepreneur, archaeologist, walking leader or author – all of these fit. I've experienced, first hand, how his approach and methodology, set out in this book, can be truly transformational. His book is a fantastic way to unlock your innate creativity. It's packed with practical tools and advice, brought to life through his own experience; wonderful, as yet untold stories of others' journeys and successes, and is relevant to all sectors of the business world. I hope you find it as insightful, inspiring, and as uplifting as I do.

Lee Mears
Partner and Executive Leadership Coach for
Preston Associates and former England and
British & Irish Lions rugby player

Introduction

'You're an idiot.'

My oldest friend often reminds me of this, usually with good reason, and over the years I've adopted it as a good filter for reflection.

Around 2015, a few years after exiting an education technology company I'd co-founded back in 1999, I decided to step out of my comfort zone and go back to my academic roots to do some postgraduate studying. To further push the boundaries of my comfort zone, I often put forward papers to be delivered at conferences. In business I'd often spoken at conferences or exhibitions and thought that I had no real fear of public speaking. I quickly learned that presenting your own academic research to a friendly, but highly critical and highly educated audience was actually terrifying. One key moment of panic seemed to be the hour or two before stepping up to the lectern, which I often spent frantically cramming, reading and re-reading my notes, looking again and again at my PowerPoint presentation and going to the bathroom far too often.

Accepted onto one of these conferences being hosted at Edinburgh University, I prepared my slides as usual, wrote my talk and booked my flight. The flight was on time arriving into Edinburgh airport and I jumped in a taxi to whisk me to a café near the University for my final preparations. I really thought I'd planned well, allowing enough time for my usual manic pre-talk cram. On this day I wasn't so lucky. Sitting in static traffic near Edinburgh Zoo, looking again and again at my watch, I eventually realized I might not make it on time so I got out of the taxi and started to walk. I walked through the streets for about an hour and a half and with minutes to spare, arrived at the conference venue, registered and went straight into a packed lecture theatre, on to the stage, plugged in my USB stick and began my presentation.

It was undoubtedly the most fluent and well-delivered one I'd ever given. The words came, my mind was focused and I answered the critical questions without hesitation. One of those questions came from Professor Colin Renfrew, Peer of the Realm, and Baron Renfrew of Kaimsthorn, the undisputed grandee and expert in the area of my research and an audience member who would have brought on a cold sweat, had I known he was there before I began.

Reflecting on this afterwards, I realized that I was an idiot. Why hadn't I done this before all those other speeches? Walking has always been a key part of my life – whether a simple dog walk, the work commute or preparing for important business meetings. I knew intuitively that walking helped me think, sparked new ways of seeing things, that it focused and organized my thoughts and put my mind in a fantastic state of clarity, but I just didn't do it enough. Walking for thinking is a blindingly obvious thing that simply works and as E.O. Wilson, the father of Biophilia (the innate human instinct to connect with nature and other forms of life) writes, 'The obvious is usually profoundly significant.'

I'm not putting myself forward as having achieved anything hugely profound nor even having had some meteoric, unicorn-wielding successes in business, and although I appreciate those who have, I am most impressed by people, regardless of career progress, who are creative, inquisitive and innovative in whatever fields they choose. As a founder of failed, successful and survivor businesses, as a mentor, non-executive director (NED), advisor and investor in others' early-stage ventures and as a lecturer in entrepreneurship, I believe that creativity is right at the heart of innovation. I believe that we all have creative agency as individuals and have a deep desire to work in highly innovative organizations and ventures and with highly creative colleagues. Creativity is at the heart of radical innovation and very much at the heart of successful entrepreneurship.

The late Dr Edward de Bono, originator of the term Lateral Thinking, who dedicated his life to inspiring, encouraging and enabling us to be better and more creative thinkers, said, 'Creative thinking is not a mystical talent. It is a skill that can be practised and nurtured.'

Every successful business is born of a unique and innovative idea, which in turn was born from the creative thinking of the people behind it. Then why is it the case that so many executives, founders and managers fail to actively develop and apply their creativity? This book aims to clarify how creativity is a key ingredient of effective leadership before highlighting the strategies and approaches through which leaders can actively develop and cultivate their creative capabilities.

Creativity leads to success by:

- Creating new ideas and developing new niches for competitive advantage;
- Applying innovative managerial strategies which cater towards the specific needs of the organization and its employees;
- Thinking of novel ways to develop your product/service and improve the business;
- Finding and recognizing patterns that lead to a greater awareness of the market/demand.

Rather than being an unchangeable trait, creativity is an ability and skill that we can train and improve. But how do you develop a creative mindset that will lead to success? Creativity doesn't tend to come from inspired 'flashes', but from sustained periods of thought and effort. Through a combined effort of both the conscious and subconscious mind, previously unseen connections can be made and original ideas flourish.

I hope my book will help you tap into your inherently creative mind and fulfil the true potential of your capabilities. *The Creativity Factor* explores the scientific and anecdotal evidence for entrepreneurial creativity and explains mechanisms, habits and techniques that increase creative thinking to help modern entrepreneurs, innovators and leaders to imagine and create real innovation through something I call 'Outside Thinking'.

From stifling work environments to repetitive schedules, I'll explore the everyday obstacles that constrain and limit our creative thinking and how we can use nature, the outdoors, walking and talking to effectively trigger and engage our mind's default mode to create real innovation.

Over the years, through trial and error, I definitely found my thinking 'space' and continue to find inspiration outside – walking in the hills, mountains and coastal paths of the UK, Europe and North Africa – with the absolute appreciation that my desk is a dangerous place from which to view the world. And I call on anyone with aspirations to be an entrepreneur, leader, fresh air thinker, idea explorer, tech innovator, creative or business *activist* to do the same.

It is time to do business differently. Take your thinking outdoors and start Outside Thinking.

CHAPTER ONE

Creativity isn't Magic

'Sit as little as possible. Give no credence to any thought that was not born outdoors while moving about freely.'

Nietzsche

I believe Friedrich Nietzsche was on to something when he made this statement and that he knew this from just doing it, practising it, making it a habit, from going outside, walking, taking in nature, wondering, pondering and thinking. Philosopher, critic, writer and philologist; the thoughts he generated on these numerous walks and went on to communicate through his work have had a profound effect on modern history, political and critical thinking. As a prolific writer, he must have spent plenty of time at his desk, but he was confident in his belief that outside was where the magic happens.

In our lives very few of us will have any profound effect on the world but we can pretty much all practise what Nietzsche did – to access the world outside of our offices and houses, walk in nature, decelerate a little and begin to generate some original and creative thoughts; deep thoughts and ideas that we can give credence to. And, if we want to generate radical innovation, become more entrepreneurial, help to bring investment to our ideas, convince people those ideas are amazing, inspire others to join our teams, build valuable ventures, influence and motivate our colleagues, staff or customers, then we have to start by being creative. We have to spark our imaginations.

If you'd like a shortcut through my book, read the following five statements, absorb them and then move on to Chapter 6 for a summary of practical tips and techniques to generate creative thinking and new ideas for yourself or within your team. The remainder of this book is full of academic research, anecdotes, interviews, actual experiences and opinions, which I hope you'll also find interesting, useful and perhaps even transformational.

> **Statement 1:** To be innovative or entrepreneurial is to be creative;
>
> **Statement 2:** Creativity is generated best through abstraction and distraction;
>
> **Statement 3:** Walking outdoors is a sure-fire way to generate creative thinking;
>
> **Statement 4:** I call this Outside Thinking;
>
> **Statement 5:** It can be truly transformational for you and your business.

Why is this? Firstly, because being entrepreneurial and being able to effectively generate the radical and innovative ideas that successful entrepreneurism requires for success is at heart a creative process. One doesn't happen successfully without the other and being creative is not the preserve of artists, poets, musicians and authors. It's in all of us and just needs to be released. A sure- and quick-fire route to release this creativity is by leaving your desk, your tech, your office and heading outside.

George Shackle's uncertainty principle

In fact, creativity isn't just useful for, it is actually a vital and essential element of entrepreneurship and heightened creativity and imagination are essential attributes for successful enterprise and entrepreneurs. This shouldn't particularly come as much of a surprise considering that progress and change have always required the imaginings of visionaries, founders, scientists and leaders. It has been the creative sparks of their imagination and, more importantly, what they did with those little sparks that has always fuelled innovation. And radical innovation is nothing new, nor is it the preserve of twenty-first century tech giants.

As far back as the 1970s, English economist George Shackle was developing rigorous theoretical frameworks on the nature of the entrepreneurial process based on the idea that business planning and innovation cannot be focused on actual, concrete knowledge of the future but instead only on one's imagination of it.

The son of a mathematics teacher, Shackle is often referred to as a post-Keynesian academic, partly perhaps influenced by his father, a mathematics teacher, who had coached a young John Maynard Keynes before his Eton days and well before he became the most famous of economists whose ideas fundamentally changed the theory and practice of macroeconomics and the economic policies of governments. The modest means of Shackle's upbringing meant that he had to put himself through university while working during the day as a bank clerk, eventually obtaining his PhD from the London School of Economics and then spending the majority of his working life as Brunner Professor of Economics at the University of Liverpool. A deep thinker, his key academic works challenged the prevailing paradigm and conventional role of probability in economics, perhaps spurred on by one of Keynes' remarks that,

by 'uncertain' knowledge ... I do not mean merely to distinguish what is known for certain from what is only probable. The game of roulette is not subject, in this sense, to uncertainty ... The sense in which I am using the term is that in which the prospect of a European war is uncertain, or the price of copper and the rate of interest 20 years hence, or the obsolescence of a new invention ... About these matters there is no scientific basis on which to form any calculable probability whatever. We simply do not know!

This view of Keynes seems to go against one of his key tenets, that people and companies tend to behave rationally. George Shackle took and ran with this concept of unknown futures to try and introduce some chaos into the economic equation.

Shackle developed a nondeterministic concept which he termed 'Bounded Uncertainty', founded on the belief that innovation – or, as he put it, 'novelty' – is an unpredictable process, chaotic and indeterminable. At its heart are the dual concepts that 'innovation is the rule, not the exception' and that 'order is the exception, not the rule'. Innovation is always happening, but we can't easily predict its turns, twists and outcomes, however much knowledge, intelligence or information we think we have. Would anyone in the early 1980s have taken seriously or foreseen the disruption that the inventor James Dyson would have on the global vacuum cleaner market, however much market analysis they'd done before he arrived on the scene? However, Shackle certainly wouldn't want us to take his work as some wishy-washy call to daydream our way to entrepreneurial success or think we'll just stumble upon innovative ideas. For a start, most of his work was based on, and applied to, monetary economics rather than to entrepreneurial activity but we can take away a central tenet summed up in this statement:

Whatever form it takes, the possession of the imaginative gift transforms the problem of accounting for human conduct.

For now, it is not a question of how given needs are satisfied. Deliberative conduct, choice, the prime economic act, depend for their possibility, when they go beyond pure instinctive animal response to stimulus, upon the conceptual power of the human mind.

The late Edward de Bono, author, physician, philosopher and originator of the term 'Lateral Thinking', perhaps puts it more succinctly as:

Radical innovation rarely comes from people set in their ways, who simply know more, or have more information, but from those who manage to generate alternative perspectives.

Finding alternative perspectives, being able to view problems in new ways or 'thinking sideways' in de Bono parlance is to be creative.

Why in God's name isn't everyone creative?

Embedded in George Shackle's work is the idea that innovation is not a simple causal process (e.g. an entrepreneur has an idea, conducts some market research, completes a business canvas, tests some ideas and then perhaps creates a successful venture) but instead is an adaptive, iterative or sometimes even chaotic process. This adaptive process is termed 'effectuation' by the academic Saras D. Sarasvathy*. Sarasvathy proposes that the creation of ventures in non-existent or non-yet-existent markets relies on focusing on what is possible, given a current, limited set of means and is actor-centric not effect-dependent. Her extensive study of successful entrepreneurs and their resultant innovations and ventures concluded that most of them strive to look for alternative perspectives rather than adopting a linear causal approach to innovation and venture building. Sarasvathy elegantly illustrates this difference between causation and effectuation by citing a chef conjuring up a meal as an example:

> By using causation the client chooses a menu in advance and the chef prepares this menu by looking for the right ingredients and following the recipes to make the dishes. In the effectual process the approach would be rather different. The client would not ask for a specific menu, but he asks the chef to make something with the ingredients available. The chef chooses one of the many different meals he is able to make with the available ingredients.

*Sarasvathy, S. (2001). 'Causation and Effectuation: Toward a Theoretical Shift from Economic Inevitability to Entrepreneurial Contingency.' *Academy of Management Review.*

The BBC series *Ready Steady Cook* and its US TV equivalent, *Ready... Set... Cook!* would lose a lot of their appeal if not based on an adaptive model.

Being able to adapt like this, or to 'effectuate' in Saras' words, to be an 'effectuator' with an aim to generate alternative perspectives to problems, for yourself and within the organizations you work for, is also the basis of social scientist Adam Grant's hugely influential book, *Originals: How Non-Conformists Move the World*, which he opens with the story of online eyewear disrupter and billion-dollar tech unicorn, Warby Parker. According to Grant, the founders of Warby Parker found both inspiration and the company name from the writing of 1950s beatnik poet and writer Jack Kerouac. Specifically, one of the founders, Dave Gilboa, was inspired by Kerouac's frequent calls to break free from social norms and go have adventures.

The story goes that one of '... our co-founder(s) Dave was wandering around the New York Public Library when he stumbled into an exhibition about Jack Kerouac. The four of us had long been inspired by Kerouac, who spurred a generation to take the road less traveled.' Dave's inspiration came chiefly from Kerouac's novel, *The Dharma Bums*, both chronologically and emotionally his semi-autobiographical follow-up to the seminal *On the Road*, which examines the duality of his time hiking and hitchhiking in the wilderness with his beatnik, late-night, Benzedrine-fuelled urban life. As entrepreneurs, perhaps we need to channel our own inner Kerouacs and explore ways to embrace the duality of our traditional work practices with all their productivity benefits and our innate sense of adventurousness in order to unlock the creativity lurking within all of us.

Certainly central to Grant's thesis is the notion that originality itself starts with being creative and he is keen to point out that his 'originals' are far more ordinary than might generally be thought. They are not necessarily serial entrepreneurs, super intelligent or extreme risk takers but simply manage somehow to find ways to see the world differently to most of us. Perhaps, then, we can say that Grant's 'originals' are not especially or naturally creative either? This is very much in line with the view of Abraham Maslow (the American psychologist best-known for creating the eponymous *Hierarchy of Needs*), who wrote, 'The key question isn't "What fosters creativity?" but it is why in God's name isn't everyone creative? Where was the human potential lost? How was it crippled? I think therefore a good question might be not why do people create, but why do people not create or innovate? We have got to abandon that sense of amazement in the face of creativity, as if it were a miracle if anybody created anything.' Grant's 'originals' aren't then starting out with any special toolkit, skills or knowledge, but have managed not to have their creativity 'crippled'.

I like to think that anyone flexing their entrepreneurial muscle is an original of some sort, whether they hit the heady heights of a Warby Parker or not. And it seems that many founders identify with these ideas too. In a recent survey I conducted of a group of founders of equity-backed, fast-growing, scale-up companies, 100 per cent of the respondents agreed with the statement 'To be innovative or entrepreneurial is to be creative.' Every one of them agreed with this, that creativity was at the heart of being entrepreneurial and the key element in innovation. Yet, on average, they rated their own creativity at just 3.6 out of 5. I wonder if this has more to do with our preconceptions about creativity and our long-held beliefs in the role of well-established and embedded processes in venture building, as opposed to the role the imagination can and should play in their success?

Confessions of a sometimes archaeologist

Now, a confession: I am an archaeologist. Before my journeys through and in the business world, I studied and practised archaeology, specializing in the Greek Bronze Age – a period in Eastern Mediterranean ancient history stretching from 3,000 to about 1,000 BCE – the era of myths, Homer, Agamemnon, art, palaces, the Minotaur and the Trojan War. This was an era of extreme risk, of setting out in sailing ships across notoriously dangerous waters to trade, forge alliances, explore and go to war. As an archaeologist I've excavated and worked on sites in the UK and Greece, excavating Greek, Iron

Age, Roman and Medieval contexts, completed a Master's in Maritime Archaeology and embarked on a PhD in Phoenician trade and commerce in the Western Mediterranean. Much of this has been done alongside my business endeavours and whilst a study of ancient history may not, at first glance, seem particularly relevant to the world of business, I have come to realize that archaeology is the king of all academic subjects and, moreover, the processes involved have had direct relevance to my work in entrepreneurship and innovation.

Archaeology is a rare, *five-dimensional* discipline – on an archaeological site we literally work in three dimensions, digging vertically and laterally through the strata of human occupation and the material culture it leaves behind: bones, pottery, buildings, weapons, coins, organic matter and, very, very occasionally, 'treasures'. The strata and contexts in which these items are found physically represent time, the fourth dimension, sometimes obvious and ordered, but more often in ways that are overlapping, confused and extremely complex to untangle and make sense of. From the complicated mix of the artefacts uncovered by the archaeology team, the location and nature of the site itself, research from other archaeological sites and the results of scientific analysis, an archaeologist must use their imagination – the fifth dimension – to try and generate a compelling narrative of what happened in the past.

Archaeology is actually a social science; the study of human behaviour through its material culture and, perhaps sadly for many onlookers, not really about treasure. The most common question I'm asked is 'What is the most exciting thing you've dug up?', to which my answer of 'Some tanning pits' generally results in disappointed faces. As archaeologists, we are never in possession of all the facts, of a complete set of information, so the precise nature of our ancient predecessors' lives cannot be really known. Instead, it must be described as best we can from a combination of this limited data we have at hand and through our imaginations, rather than actual, concrete knowledge of the past. Our job as archaeologists is to combine data and our imagination to tell a compelling story to our extremely critical academic colleagues. Funny how this pretty much mirrors the exact same process of building your deck and business plan and pitching your start-up to an investor! These business plans include a limited set of data and loads of assumptions wrapped up in, hopefully, a compelling and convincing story that we have used our creativity and imaginations to shape and develop.

My archaeological training and experience have stood me in good stead, both in the trench and in the meeting room. I now take a wide view of creativity: it's not reserved for art school graduates, writers or performers, but available to all of us to put to use. As Edward de Bono put it: 'There is no doubt that creativity is the most important human resource of all. Without creativity, there would be no progress, and we would be forever repeating the same patterns.' However important to humankind and culture, progress is not driven by art. It's driven by innovation and innovation is driven by creativity. And that's been true since well before those Greeks set out on their heavy-laden sailing ships on Homer's 'wine-dark sea'.

We are all inherently creative

Creativity and play are intertwined and come naturally to us when we're children. Perhaps the most ubiquitous of toys, LEGO, exemplifies this and way back in the 1970s, their packaging stated, 'The urge to create is equally strong in all children. Boys and girls. It's imagination that counts. Not skill. You build whatever comes into your head, the way you want it. A bed or a truck. A doll's house or a spaceship. A lot of boys like doll's houses. They're more human than spaceships. A lot of girls prefer spaceships. They're more exciting than doll's houses. The most important thing is to put the right material in their hands and let them create whatever appeals to them.' In other words, regardless of gender, we all start out naturally curious and creative and don't give a damn about stereotypes.

As we are all inherently creative, we can also all be entrepreneurial. Guided by his work studying the prevalence and characteristics of successful entrepreneurs, Per Davidsson of Queensland University of Technology Business concluded: 'No psychological or sociological characteristics have been found which predict with high accuracy that someone will become an entrepreneur or excel at entrepreneurship', and, suggests that, 'the research based evidence suggests that people faced with an opportunity that suits them, and in interaction with people with complementary skills, most people would be able to pursue a successful career as entrepreneurs'. Or, as Maslow might have put it – why in God's name isn't everyone an entrepreneur? If we can all be creative and all have the chance to be entrepreneurial, is it just that some people don't notice, or choose not to act on opportunities that present themselves?

Much has written about opportunity-based theories, championed especially by the late Peter Drucker, who was often described as 'the founder of modern management'. These theories tend to focus on how to spot and then exploit new opportunities and are centred on the concept that the opportunities exist in-potentia waiting to be *discovered*. Primarily process-orientated, focused on a methodical analysis of opportunities, testing and implementation, these theories are widely adopted in large organizations as an accepted framework for innovation management. Drucker himself worked with some of the biggest US corporations of his time – General Motors, IBM, General Electric – and was somewhat legendary in post-war Japan's fast-growing business environment. Accepting that opportunities do exist in-potentia, waiting to be 'discovered' and that the process of identification and analysis is vital, something is still missing

– a leap of imagination, a vision of a solution no one else has seen, one that could perhaps prove outlandishly successful.

It is generally recognized, both in academic circles and in the commercial world, that imagination is essential to entrepreneurship or innovation, but not particularly understood. At the same time, they are rarely acknowledged or integrated into these traditional models of innovation, which tend to ignore the difficult 'messy' nature of creativity, be somewhat processual in nature and are often built on the work of people like Drucker.

Taking all this as her starting point, Sara Elias and some of her academic colleagues* set out to empirically map or measure the role played by imaginations in innovation. They tried to build a more robust model for entrepreneurship that directly accepted this non-linear reality and the notion that 'novel ideas emerge from (un)conscious processes'. Key to their work is the acceptance that imagination can be a conscious, unconscious, self-reflective and an embodied process. It's not just dreaming or thinking, but in action should involve things like sketching, building, playing, having conversations and making connections in the real, physical world. Which, of course, sounds very much like the experience of a small child playing LEGO with friends.

*Chiles, T., Crawford, B., Elias, S. 'Entrepreneurial Imagining: How a small team of arts entrepreneurs created the world's largest traveling carillon.' *Organisational Studies*, July 2021.

In the work of Elias, this idea is exemplified by the statement that 'The narratives that [are generally told about] entrepreneurs typically emphasize triumphs, but entrepreneurs themselves may be scarred by the process of starting, failing, starting over, and repeating, all before attaining success. By embracing complexities and avoiding linear entrepreneurial stories, as sometimes appears in process models, our model captures insights into futures that never became.' The perhaps visually inelegant model they propose – no simple graphs for them – is based on the botanical rhizome, a sort of 'image of thought' that allows a very organic visualization of the entrepreneurial process with the role of imagination baked right in. The model is built on five key elements:

- Experiencing;
- Early Creating;
- Reaching an Impasse and Gestating;
- (Re)creating and Valuating Imaging Futures;
- Choosing and Enterprising.

Together, according to Elias and her colleagues, these allow ideas to evolve, shoot off at tangents and be abandoned but not forgotten, but in the end be a part of progress towards real innovation.

This 'rhizomatic' approach is informed by the pedagogical work of Gilles Deleuze and Félix Guattari, who, inspired by a type of plant stem, the rhizome, used the term in their book *A Thousand Plateaus** to refer to networks that establish connections between organizations – in politics, sciences and arts – that have no apparent order. As they explain: 'The underground sprout of a rhizome does not have a traditional root. There is a stem there, the oldest part of which dies off while simultaneously rejuvenating itself at the tip. The rhizome's renewal of itself proceeds autopoietically: the new relations generated via rhizomatic connections are not copies, but each and every time a new map, a cartography. A rhizome does not consist of units, but of dimensions and directions.' An autopoietic (I had to look it up too) system is one that produces and reproduces its own elements as well as its own structures.

What I like about these models is that they allow a much broader and nuanced exploratory, imaginative and playful phase in creativity and innovation. This is very much how a non-business focused, creative-orientated process might look, and a far cry from most of the process-driven models routinely used in businesses. Perhaps these phases of creative discovery and playfulness come naturally and comfortably to successful founders and innovators? Perhaps these innovators simply never lost the child in them and have metaphorically just carried on playing LEGO with their friends?

*Deleuze, G., Guattari, F. (2013). *A Thousand Plateaus: Capitalism and Schizophrenia*. Bloomsbury Academic.

There are no unique ideas

I've spoken to many investors about what they look for or see in the founders of ventures they choose to invest in and how important these aspects are when making investment decisions. They often cite a similar range of personality traits as being of key importance; traits such as grit, resilience, self-awareness and a thirst for knowledge. But they also look for people who can spot the subtle differences in the opportunities visible to many. Will Herman, co-author (with Rajat Bhargava) of *The Startup Playbook: Founder-to-Founder Advice from Two Startup Veterans* and serial entrepreneur himself, says, 'I just don't believe that there are that many unique ideas and that the uniqueness of your idea really isn't that important.' So, it's not necessarily about the idea itself being new or unique, but about being able to creatively exploit the idea. This is the creative leap of imagination we're seeking.

'My dear, everything is a remix, a compilation, a mix-tape. There is nothing new in art except talent. There is nothing new in art except in the way the puzzle pieces are put together. For the great thing about the puzzle pieces of art is that there are paradoxically no edges and all edges at the same time. Everything connects yet doesn't. The most valuable thing in art isn't the content, it's the artist's eye', so might have written the great Russian playwright and author Anton Chekhov if writing today, suggests one anonymous online writer, building on Chekhov's actual quote: 'There is nothing new in art except talent.' Maybe then the most valuable thing in innovation isn't the opportunity, it's the entrepreneur's talent, or eye?

In 2004 the Royal College of Art in London decided to develop this artistic view of innovation into commercially exploitable reality. Realizing that few other areas or disciplines of academic study took the trouble to help students learn how to generate original ideas, they decided that the training and courses they offered should and could lead to real entrepreneurial success for students. By 2019 this resulted in McKinsey & Company labelling their InnovationRCA programme a 'world-class spinout incubator and an inspirational organization acting as a significant driver of entrepreneurial growth, delivering impressive results'. The Royal College of Art programme's success lay in managing to see the view of the entrepreneur through artists' eyes.

To stand a chance as successful innovators or entrepreneurs we must all be, or learn to be, creative, whether we're art or business school graduates or never graduated at all. The good news is that we all can be. I've worked with hundreds of companies and there is no doubt that creativity is more often suppressed than supported. This is not because new ideas aren't valued, but the suppression is generally unintentional: the systemic structures and environments we tend to work in, designed to focus on key business factors such as productivity, finance and control, can make it difficult for creative approaches to flourish and often end up limiting innovation and new, radical ideas.

Inspiration through distraction

Systemic works structures, busy-ness and the over-control of our time can be key limiting factors to allowing creativity to flourish, but, conversely, innovation might also be limited by simply doing nothing or resting and hoping this alone will spark some new ideas. Inspiration is first and foremost generated through mental distraction. Anecdotally, there are plenty of examples of new ideas generated while the thinker is engaged in an entirely unrelated activity and this is something we've probably all experienced at some point. These may appear to be 'ah-ha' or 'eureka' moments but in reality have been gestating, albeit consciously and subconsciously, for some time.

In 2012, psychologist Benjamin Baird* and some colleagues set out to empirically test, for the first time, the role of distraction in creativity through a highly ingenious experiment they devised. Initially, 145 participants were asked to complete a benchmark creativity test called the 'Unusual Uses Task', in which the aim is to find as many surprising uses for a common

---

*Baird B., Smallwood J., Mrazek M.D., Kam J.W.Y., Franklin M.S., Schooler J.W. (2012). 'Inspired by Distraction: Mind Wandering Facilitates Creative Incubation.' *Psychological Science*. 23(10):1117–1122.

object as possible. For example, a coffee cup might produce a list like this:

- Plant pot;
- Soup bowl;
- Pen holder;
- Scoop for dried feed;
- Template for drawing a circle;
- A spider trap;
- A paint mixing pot;
- Candle holder;
- Cupcake mould;
- Beer flagon for a band of Viking elves;
- And so on ...

When the participants had completed this task, Baird and his team split them into three groups. Some were allowed to rest and relax, others were given a relatively undemanding task to do and the remaining participants were asked to tackle a more complex task, all for a period of 12 minutes. At the end of this period, all of the participants returned to the unusual uses test and their results in both rounds of the test were rated and compared for:

- fluency (the total number of alternative uses);
- originality (how unusual the answers were);

- flexibility (the breadth of categories covered); and
- elaboration (the amount of detail given).

The results were striking. There was a 40 per cent improvement in creative problem solving and idea incubation in the group engaged in the undemanding task over those who were doing the demanding task, simply resting or taking a break. This may seem surprising, but Baird and colleagues argue that, with no distraction, our thoughts tend to revert to a logical, sequential pattern basis while, if our brains are challenged with a complex task, there simply isn't scope for creativity. Being actively distracted is the sweet spot for creativity to flourish and it's not a marginal 1 per cent gain, it's a whopping 40 per cent.

Many years before, Freud had coined the phrase 'infantile thought without merit', which aligns with the state of mind-wandering that Baird was investigating. Alongside Baird's work, modern neuroscience research is dramatically rewriting and overturning Freud's viewpoint. Some of this neuroscientific work has shown that it is a very natural state and that we all do it for ridiculous amounts of time. In fact, a paper by Harvard psychologists Daniel Gilbert and Matthew A. Killingsworth[*] found that we all spend, on average, 46.9 per cent of our waking

---

[*]Gilbert, D.T., Killingsworth, M.A. (2010). 'A Wandering Mind Is an Unhappy Mind.' *Science* 330, 932.

time with our minds in this state. The only real exception was when making love. That, we focus on, apparently!

Other studies* uncovered that mind-wandering and daydreaming are not useless or mindless states as Freud believed, but actually vital to some important cognitive functions, showing that that those of us who consistently and consciously engage in mind-wandering tend to score better in almost all and any measures of creativity. The trick to using mind-wandering effectively and creatively to our advantage is to manage to maintain some sort of meta-awareness while we do it, and not to simply drift off into our imaginations. Mind-wandering is ubiquitous in humans and something we can all access, but we need something, a distraction, as Baird would have it, to be able to make effective use of it and to productively channel our wandering minds towards useful creativity.

The leading principle in Julia Cameron's best-selling 1992 book, *The Artist's Way: A Spiritual Path to Higher Creativity*†,

*Christoff, K., Gordon, A. M., Smallwood, J., Smith, R., & Schooler, J. W. (2009). 'Experience sampling during fMRI reveals default network and executive system contributions to mind wandering.' *Proceedings of the National Academy of Sciences, USA*, 106, 8719–8724, and, Smallwood, J., Nind, L., & O'Connor, R. C. (2009). 'When is your head at? An exploration of the factors associated with the temporal focus of the wandering mind.' *Consciousness and Cognition*, 18, 118–125.
†Cameron, J. (1992). *The Artist's Way: A Spiritual Path to Higher Creativity*. Macmillan.

a sort of blueprint and manual for creative inspiration used and lauded by artists, film-makers, actors and more for over 30 years, is that, 'Creativity is the natural order of life. Life is energy – pure creative energy.' Cameron, often referred to as 'The Godmother' of creativity (apparently, and somewhat disappointingly, not inspired by her marriage to *Goodfellas* director, Martin Scorsese) believes – very much like Maslow – that there is no such thing as a creative elite; rather, creativity is fundamental to us all as human beings. She thinks that perhaps we simply lose creative confidence as we age and mature, or that the belief is somehow drilled out of us. The late educationalist Sir Ken Robinson would certainly agree with Cameron that our education systems tend to drill creativity out of us and he proposed as much in his seminal – and most watched ever – TED Talk, *Do Schools Kill Creativity?*

Julia Cameron's latest book, *The Listening Path: The Creative Art of Attention** revisits some of her favourite creative techniques but, notably, she now promotes using walking 'to induce "aha" moments of insight'. One of her key tenets is this: to induce these insights through walking, you need to listen to others, yourself, the environment around you and even to silence. Through her own practices and reflections, Cameron developed her 'walking-to-listen' approach to creativity after moving over a decade ago

*Cameron, J. (2021). *The Listening Path: The Creative Art of Attention.* Macmillan.

to the mountains above Santa Fe in New Mexico. Here, away from the 'honking, sirens and whistles' of Manhattan, she could 'hear' what she should be doing next.

Walking to listen, to manage and harness our mind-wandering thoughts and walking to think creatively are central to my practice and to this book's core thesis and it seems I'm on to nothing particularly new here. So why is it that we rarely give these superpowers we naturally possess the time they require?

Stop sleepworking

Too many of us are guilty of what I call 'sleepworking'. I don't mean this as a particularly derogatory term, but one that suggests we rarely question deeply why or how things are done in our working lives and environments. That doesn't mean we don't do good or productive work but we are often stuck on process tracks that rarely allow creativity to thrive or new ideas to be sparked, discussed and explored. Many individuals long to be entrepreneurs and every venture would love their staff to be more entrepreneurial, but few support this with suitable resources or rewards. Every one of us possesses the creative powers to generate new ideas and act on them, but few actually do. Businesses and organizations rarely give the time and space for extensive idea generation and often race to find ideas that are quickly and easily implemented and managed. This might lead to getting new products to market, increased productivity, and profitability, but is unlikely to lead to radical innovation. Through nurturing, engaging and developing our imaginations, we should be able to do better than adapt to markets, trends or customer needs instead shaping them to our own ideas and desires.

Don't we all wish to think the unthinkable, to find obscure ideas, to take flights of imaginative fancy, to not be run-of-the-mill and think not just outside the box, but so far from the box that we can't even see the box anymore? To do this, we have to find ways to unlock, play and experiment with our innate creativity. This isn't something we should do in our spare time, at an annual strategy meeting in a boardroom, being forced to do some blue-sky thinking. It is deep work and should be given the space and time to flourish. Creating, playing and even bunking off can be, counterintuitively, a very productive endeavour. The outdoors is an enormous, beautiful, varied sandbox of possibility for unleashing this creative thinking. Once you've seen the panelled rooms of one English country house converted into a corporate away-day venue you've seen them all, yet out there in the wild there are not only all the glories of the natural world, but also other, exceptional places to rest your head, body and mind – mountain-top bothies, cabins deep in the forest and wild campsites by remote lakes. These are the places where deep work can happen so why don't you just turn off your PowerPoint and go and do something less boring instead? You won't find your competitive edge at the bottom of an Excel spreadsheet, however large you project it. And even if you're not bored, you won't be innovative sitting in a boardroom, however nice the wallpaper.

Five Walks That Changed My Thinking

1. Kinder Scout, Derbyshire, UK, 1974

As a kid, the only holidays we ever took were camping – and we did a lot of it. Never abroad and rarely to anywhere particularly touristy, more likely a remote field in a National Park with very limited equipment – no camping chairs for us, me, my brother and sister sleeping inches apart on rudimentary and often leaky airbeds. I don't remember my first camping trips, but having two older siblings, I was certainly well accustomed to them as an infant. Then aged almost five, we travelled north from southern England to the Peak District, where we set up camp near Edale in the heart of these rugged mountains.

Having pitched the heavy canvas tent, a plan was made for the next day: my dad and older brother, Nick, would climb Kinder Scout, the highest point in the park. Mum, my sister, Caroline, and I would walk to the trail head, wave them on their way and return to hang out at the camp and await their return. But I just kept going, Dad's walking stick in hand, refusing offers of shoulder rides or chances to turn back. Having reached the summit, I returned to camp all under my own steam. I was apparently so elated that I didn't stop there, but donned my dad's rucksack, picked up his stick again and said I was setting out to find fish and chips for the family.

To be honest, I don't actually remember the climb, camp or even the trip itself, but over the years, my family have retold the story and shown the few fuzzy photos enough times that I feel I do remember it. I'm sure many people as young as me have made their own – epic for them – early journeys, but for me it certainly meant something and started a love affair with walking, mountains and the outdoors. And, perhaps, those early outdoors experiences unknowingly inspired in me a strong sense of determination.

CHAPTER TWO

To Innovate is to be Creative

'What is the most resilient parasite? Bacteria? A virus? An intestinal worm? An idea. Resilient... highly contagious. Once an idea has taken hold of the brain it's almost impossible to eradicate. An idea that is fully formed – fully understood – that sticks; right in there somewhere.'

Dominick Cobb (played by Leonardo DiCaprio) in *Inception*

Hopefully, it is blindingly obvious, complete common sense and we can all agree that new ideas are central to entrepreneurship, successful innovation and to human and technological progress and always have been. They spark conversation, experimentation, exploration, launch ventures, whether eventually successful or not, fuel change and pivots, generate value, excite investors and sometimes destroy competition or create entirely new markets. But ideas are nothing like other resources in the arsenals of founders, ventures and organizations. They're not like capital, people, banks, management consultants, support services, incubators or accelerators, partnerships or plant, but they are still vital for ventures of all scales to succeed, grow and to innovate.

Putting aside any ethical concerns, the technology isn't there yet for us to infiltrate people's dreams and steal their ideas as Dominick Cobb excelled at in the movie *Inception*, but entrepreneurs, leaders, executives and at least some of their teams need to be able to generate and spot good ideas, to be able to explore them, discard them, park or, when right, develop and profit from them.

It would also seem intuitive to assume that intelligence and experience would correlate with successful leadership in these areas, i.e. that experienced, clever people are more likely to have new ideas and have the skills to exploit them. However, research has shown that successful venture leaders simply tend to be the people who come up with good solutions to problems rather than necessarily being great idea creators or spotters. If this is so, then the issue is that to be able to think about and come up with these good solutions, existing and aspiring leaders require regular exposure to good ideas.

Related research showed that the divergent (or creative) thinking traits displayed by a group of successful leaders did exert unique effects on creative problem-solving tasks but that this could not be attributed to any measure of their intelligence or expertise. Those who are good and practised at divergent thinking do tend to come up with more, good ideas and it turns out that leaders who are good at this are also great at finding solutions to act on, i.e. to exploit and profit from them. This is a heady mix for potential entrepreneurs to strive for, or, more practically, to practice and make themselves better at doing. When I talk to investors about their processes of choosing the right investments, emphasis is quite often put on a founder's, or leadership team's experience and intelligence, but perhaps more weight should be put on, or they should be testing, a founding team's creativity regardless of track record or academic prowess. So firstly, let's debunk some of the myths of entrepreneurship and the traits that successful entrepreneurs are sometimes said to have:

- Entrepreneurs are born, not made;
- Entrepreneurs need to be extroverts;
- Entrepreneurs should do everything in their business;
- Entrepreneurship is a linear journey;
- Entrepreneurs have no time for friends, family or fun;
- All you need is a good idea.

Let's reframe those:

- Entrepreneurs are made, not born – it's a craft you can learn and master;
- Entrepreneurs don't need to be extroverts – you just need imagination and we all have that;
- Entrepreneurs should never do everything in their business – collective creativity is the key;

- Entrepreneurship is always a non-linear journey – embrace this and you'll keep innovating;
- Entrepreneurs must find time for friends, family and fun – it's never just about the money;
- A good idea is just the start – hopefully, this book will help with that bit!

There are certainly many successful entrepreneurs out there who, on paper, didn't seem to display the qualifications of 'intelligence' or the experience that investors seem to be looking for.

Jonny takes a leap into the unknown

At school in the 1980s, Jonny Ohlson may certainly have questioned his teacher's belief in his own intelligence as the establishment tried to squeeze him through a narrow, academically-focused curriculum window and ended up spitting him out into the newly formed 'Z' class for educational lost causes. But it was here – free to explore what at the time were 'unimportant', unacademic subjects, such as art and design and allowed to simply 'mess around a lot' – that Ohlson discovered his own creativity. After leaving school, he put this to good use in the world of advertising, joining Saatchi & Saatchi in their 1980s heyday as a junior creative, when they produced what is considered to be their most breakthrough creative work – for the British Conservative Party, Silk Cut cigarettes, British Airways, Club 18–30 and others – eventually rising through the ranks to become a board director. Possibly a natural step for a man central to London's fashionable media crowd, Ohlson then collaborated with Soho House founder Nick Jones, becoming instrumental in its expansion into a global brand, with outposts across Europe, the US and Asia.

By the mid-2000s, successful, experienced and connected, most corporate investors would have jumped at the chance to back Jonny Ohlson if he'd decided to launch his own agency or venture further into the creative industries. He obviously had the experience and was highly intelligent, whatever his exam certificates said. But Ohlson took a broader view of 'creative industries' and was about to personally *pivot* in a major way.

Fascinated by the Human Genome Project, an international scientific research project with the goal of determining the base pairs that make up human DNA, and of identifying, mapping and sequencing all of the genes of the human genome, Ohlson was becoming more and more interested in what at the time was fringe science and he became convinced that DNA would be the defining technology of the twenty-first century, much as computer coding and algorithms had become to define innovation in the later twentieth century. He knew literally nothing about the field or the science, and certainly was not a white-coated scientific boffin with a PhD, but driven by his conviction, he tracked down, met, got talking to and personally financed the salaries some people who were better placed to understand the sector. Soon he'd turned his back on the world of advertising and, in 2008, Touchlight Genetics was born.

Touchlight created new and innovative techniques and processes to make synthetic DNA at speed and scale in order to support the enormous growth in genetic medicine development that was under way. Since being founded on Ohlson's dollar, they've raised a further $125m in investment without having to approach a traditional venture capitalist or funder, rapidly achieved the magic $1 billion unicorn valuation status and have built state-of-the-art labs in a former waterworks on the outskirts of London – all of which allows a large staff of scientists to be 'creative'.

I use this last word carefully here as Jonny Ohlson and his team didn't built a biotech firm from any existing blueprint or a tried-and-tested model for ventures in this sector. In fact, the business is more akin to an advertising agency, both physically and operationally. Jonny prides himself on recruiting the best possible scientific talent, offering them the lab of their dreams, letting them all share financially in the success and, most importantly, giving them 'briefs' (as you would a creative team at an agency) and plenty of time and then waiting to see what they create. He truly believes that the creative thinking and processes vital to venture building are the same whether applied at the cutting edge of science or to consumer advertising. And this culture of creativity is paying dividends, both metaphorically, in recruitment and in revenues, and also literally in the valuation of Touchlight.

Ohlson thought and stepped his way sideways out of the creative industries and into a world of innovation. One UK government definition of the creative industries he left behind is, 'those based on individual creativity, skill and talent, or which have the potential to create wealth and jobs through the development or production of intellectual property', which aligns pretty much perfectly with the Touchlight way, even if as an innovative biotech firm, they are unlikely to win a Clio (the annual awards recognizing innovation and creative excellence in advertising) at next year's advertising awards ceremony.

Originality is overrated

I wonder if many venture capitalists would have backed Jonny Ohlson in a market he knew nothing about, had no experience of and, at the outset at least, didn't really even have much of a plan for? Joe Stringer, a partner at Octopus Ventures (one of the largest and most active venture investors in Europe, with over £1.7bn under management, who since 2008 have backed over 130 teams, including Zoopla Property Group, Secret Escapes, Depop and Cazoo) would probably be a fan of Touchlight as he is a firm believer that creativity plays a vital role in the execution, growth and success of good ventures, and not only in the formation of the original idea itself. When we think about this it seems obvious. Few of the most successful ventures or companies were born out of some totally new idea or product, but through doing something differently and, or, better. As the American writer and humourist Mark Twain said, 'There is no such thing as a new idea. It is impossible. We simply take a lot of old ideas and put them into a sort of mental kaleidoscope. We give them a turn and they make new and curious combinations.'

So, are there really no original ideas left? Getting into arguments about whether this is actually true or false is generally not a fruitful avenue unless you're a fan of late-night, perhaps wine-fuelled, philosophical discussions – and who isn't? However, it can be a fruitless endeavour because it's just too hard to reach any meaningful conclusion. Try thinking of something that is truly not derivative of something that existed before. If you can, is it possible to describe it with only reference to itself, without using any metaphors? That would be original in the truest sense. Start-up pitches today are awash with metaphors, giving away perhaps their lack of true originality – 'we're the UBER of X', for example. In September 2016, *WIRED* magazine calculated that 526 pitch decks available at that time on AngelList (the best known US website for start-ups and investors to find each other) included the term 'Uber for' in their descriptions. The X idea in some of these may well be highly creative but it's hardly original.

When used as a noun, 'creativity' means the ability to use imagination to produce a novel idea or product that is useful to society, whereas 'originality' means the quality of being original or novel. Two definitions* of creativity are:

'The production of ideas and objects that are both novel or original and worthwhile or appropriate, that is, useful, attractive, meaningful, or correct.'

and,

'The ability to transcend traditional ideas, rules, patterns, relationships, or the like, and to create meaningful new ideas, forms, methods, interpretations.'

And originality is defined[†] as being:

'The quality of being new and interesting in a way that is different from anything that has existed before.'

Striving to be original is hard, perhaps almost impossible, but aiming to be creative, to be able to transcend existing norms, bend the rules, see new patterns and come up with new ideas is within anyone's grasp. It just takes a little effort and practice.

*Oxford Reference (Oxford University Press) & The Standard Webster's Dictionary
†Collins English Dictionary

There are no eureka moments

Do you recognize the brands DMOZ or Archie, or remember early internet ventures such as Ask Jeeves or Excite? The earliest search engines, generally built for academic uses, predated the World Wide Web and were followed rapidly by plenty of commercial ones during the 1990s. They were all battling for the attention of a group first identified by academic librarian Jean Armour Polly – 'surfers' – but then Google came along and just did it all better. Social Media has existed from the late 1990s, through sites such as Six Degrees, followed by Myspace in the early 2000s, but in 2004 Facebook came along and took it all mainstream and on to everyone's device.

During the early and mid-1990s, I worked for a now mostly-forgotten, multi-billion-dollar, fast-scaling, acquisitive company based out of a nondescript office block off I95 in Connecticut, US, selling computer hardware and software online and via frequently distributed mail-order catalogues, but it was Amazon who went on to create the dominant all-in-one online shop we know today. Yet Amazon's Jeff Bezos, Facebook's Mark Zuckerberg and Google co-founders Larry Page and Sergey Brin are routinely described as original thinkers and visionaries. In his 2017 Harvard graduation address, Zuckerberg explained that we shouldn't trust the idea of innovation that Hollywood puts forth, that there are no single eureka moments. He went on to outline how he encourages creativity in the Facebook workforce, which we'll return to in Chapter 4 (*see also* page 106). The takeaway here is that the outcome of creativity isn't necessarily originality. If we focus on trying to be original, we'll likely fail; if we concentrate on being creative, we'll all be rewarded.

Artists understand that nothing is really original, are completely comfortable continually building on what has gone before and become unburdened by the freedom this gives them to concentrate on simply being creative. In perhaps the best book ever written (or perhaps drawn?) on this subject, *Steal Like an Artist: 10 Things Nobody Told You About Being Creative*[*], Austin Kleon says, 'Every artist gets asked the question, "Where do you get your ideas?". The honest artist answers, "I steal them."' And, as John Maynard Keynes may have replied to Kleon, the real 'difficulty lies not so much in developing new ideas as in escaping from old ones'. Studying, analyzing and stealing from existing products, services and ideas is a good thing, if (and it's an important *if*) we give ourselves the tools, time, freedom and permission to properly invest time in creativity.

In reality, what most entrepreneurs and organizations are looking for in fact is innovation, not originality. And companies will end up innovating more frequently if the individuals working within them think more creatively, by being encouraged and supported to look at problems or

[*]Kleon, A. (2012). *Steal Like an Artist: 10 Things Nobody Told You About Being Creative*. Workman.

opportunities from different perspectives. If we take J. Daniel Couger's* rather dull definition on innovation from his 1995 book, *Creative Problem Solving and Opportunity Finding*, as 'the process by which new ideas are put into practice', then what we're really searching for are *new* ideas, not necessarily hugely original but certainly ones generated through being creative.

Assuming we have generated one of these new ideas, exploring it and putting it into practice is a whole different thing and then making a success of that something else altogether. But, investing loads of time in the process of trying to make it happen is likely to be an entirely fruitless endeavour if we haven't put proper effort into generating good, new ideas.

Back to the future

Let's wind the clock back to 2004. Zuckerberg and friends had just unleashed his rudimentary TheFacebook onto an unsuspecting student body at Harvard, Mozilla's opensource Firefox browser was starting to give Microsoft's incumbent and generally auto-installed Internet Explorer some serious competition, second generation iPods had added video capabilities, an MP3 player and iTunes were launched, SKYPE owned the infant voice over internet (IP) market, mobile phones could at last live up to the claim to be pocket

*Couger, J.D. (1995). *Creative Problem Solving and Opportunity Finding*. Boyd and Fraser Publishing.

computers and 'Blogging' was crowned Word of the Year by US dictionary publisher, Merriam-Webster. Looking back at the venture landscape of the early 2000s now, of the top ten fastest-growing tech companies of the year 2004, only e-Bay is still a recognizable brand to most people. Innovation does drive change; these changes can be rapid and monumental, but each step on this journey starts with a new idea.

I've had the pleasure myself, over the years, of working for some people worthy of the title of 'visionary' and probably chief among those was Chris Anderson, now of TED fame. Known as a serial entrepreneur, social entrepreneur and philanthropist, Anderson first founded Future Publishing in the early 1990s on the back of an idea, a vision and a small bank loan. Future grew into, and continues to be, one of the largest and most innovative magazine and content publishers on the planet.

Anderson is now one of the chief architects and proponents of what he calls radical generosity – key to TED's free-for-all approach – which I believe the genesis of which was already in place in those early days. Not that he gave content away then, but in the 'idea factory' that Future was from the outset. He managed to instil in staff across all of the publishing disciplines the belief that anything is possible and that everyone's ideas are valued. In this way he was radically generous in his leadership, to which the generation of new ideas and the power of individual and collective imagination were central.

In 2019, Anderson was awarded an honorary degree from the University of Bath, the city in which Future Publishing was and is still based. He opened his acceptance speech with these words: 'If you talk about the power of ideas, if we could see and map the ideas that are bubbling in each of these minds right here, if you could really see them, you would have a glimpse of what the future is going to be like.' If that's not the view of a visionary, I don't know what is, but it also embodies George Shackle's theory that you can't see it or predict it, but can only imagine those futures.

The idea isn't everything

Although never ascending close to the heady achievements that Chris Anderson has achieved to date, my wife, Siobhain, and I had, a few years after leaving Chris's Future Publishing to work in the early e-commerce world in Connecticut for a while, co-founded one of the earliest education technology start-ups out of our spare bedroom in the World Heritage Georgian city of Bath, in the south-west of the UK. Conceived late one evening lounging on a Thai beach after six months of round-the-world freewheeling and backpacking, on our return, and driven primarily through lack of start-up funds, our business was founded on harvesting, editing and sharing, via a freemium model, user-generated teaching and learning material produced by school teachers across the country.

By 2004, pretty much every secondary school teacher in the UK, and plenty around the world, used our service. We had a nice office, a growing body of lovely staff, traditional publishers were sniffing around our 'interesting' digital venture and we had recently been kicked off hosting companies' platforms for 'using all their bandwidth'. Everything we did was online and the online world still felt a bit like the Wild West. When we did go out to conferences and meet our customers, they either thought we were a one-man band, or filled some massive tower block of office space in London. Through necessity (there were no easy off-the-shelf Software as a Service (SaaS) products to find and subscribe to back then), we'd built from scratch our own fully online publishing and document management system, customer support services and file management to deal with documents we published and the customers we serviced. We had thousands of documents sitting in the 'cloud' and tens of thousands of users accessing and downloading them every day, so the stakes were high. The solution to our bandwidth problem involved buying our own servers, convincing our software development partners to house them for us and arranging to have their car park excavated to install a new physical, dedicated pipe connected across it to the local telephone company's regional switch. We had to innovate to survive and to meet our customers' needs.

Coupled to this, as the commercial half of our husband and wife 'executive' team, I was running around the country visiting schools, conferences, publishers and potential partners. Returning on a then WiFi-less train from London late one day, I was attempting to work, sat in front of my laptop, my BlackBerry connecting it to the latest, albeit intermittent, 3G connection, looking out of the window as the rainy Berkshire fields swept past. At the time this seemed quite magical – I was travelling a high speed, I was online, our servers were delivering quickly. I had the files I'd saved on my computer and I could see our site online, login, access some parts of our remote system, but it didn't really all join up and was a somewhat frustrating experience. What I really needed was all the files I might want to access, whether on my laptop or on our servers, accessible from wherever and whenever I was, and to be able to download, edit, upload, publish or share them on the fly. So that's the system we specified and had built by our development team. And it worked brilliantly. Brilliantly enough that we decided to offer the same service and functionality to all of our members for free. Me, my wife, our staff and teachers across the country could now create, edit, save, organize, access, share, present and project onto whiteboards in their classrooms all of our content, stuff they'd found online, documents they'd edited and any of their own they wished to add. At a time when interactive whiteboards were rapidly being installed in classrooms across the country this seemed like magic and an enormous technological step forward for teachers. I could also access our own systems and my personal files wherever I happened to be on my travels.

Teachers loved it, I loved it, our staff loved in. We felt great about our idea and innovation, congratulated ourselves that it had improved our retention rates by over 5 per cent, but didn't realize in the slightest the wider commercial potential it offered and we didn't call it Dropbox. In 2007, on a campus at MIT, Drew Houston – frustrated by very similar things – did.

So, I invented Dropbox. In reality, there were probably hundreds of people frustrated by the same limitations I was and plenty of proto-Dropboxes out there. I've included my story to highlight the links from idea to innovation to exploitation. Missing out on the successful exploitation and billions of dollars end is something of course, but having the initial idea is everything. Without it, we'll never innovate and we'll never have a chance to exploit it, or to achieve what Drew did.

Where can these innovative or new ideas come from? In the world of fiction writing, the author Christopher Booker believes that there are only seven basic story plots:

- Overcoming the Monster (*The Magnificent Seven, Star Wars*);
- Rags to Riches (*Cinderella, Jane Eyre*);
- The Quest (*Lord of the Rings, Raiders of The Lost Ark*);
- Voyage and Return (*The Lion King, Back to the Future*);
- Rebirth (*Groundhog Day, The Frog Prince*);
- Comedy (*Much Ado about Nothing, The Big Lebowski*); and finally,
- Tragedy (*Romeo and Juliet, The Great Gatsby*).

Authors and directors may bring unlimited creativity and vision to their characters, scenes, dialogue, cinematography and direction, but, if you agree with Booker, all of their narratives are born of these overarching structures. Similarly, the consensus of the start-up and venture capital worlds seems to be that there might only be seven distinct sources of potentially good ideas for new ventures. Let's explore each of them as potential sources of inspiration for start-up ideas. You can use these to think *seriously* about ideas you might want to explore, as mental exercises to simply start exploring your potential as an entrepreneur, or with your colleagues and teams as a good starter exercise on innovation thinking.

No. 1: We (Could) Rule at This

What are you, your colleagues, friends, team really, REALLY good at? In considering this question, can you identify ideas that you would just kill at and where you would have an instant unfair advantage over any competitors? The beauty of this source of ideas is that you rapidly answer a question any early-stage venture should ask itself (and one any investor certainly will) – is there a good founder/market fit? To start to generate ideas you can think about companies you've worked at, jobs you've had, what worked, what didn't and so on.

Digital Ocean founded in 2012 is now one of the cloud's biggest hosting companies and that's in a sector with players such as Microsoft and Google. Now with customers in 185 countries, they've raised almost $500m in funding over the last eight years, primarily as they have always had fantastic founder-market fit. The founding brothers, Ben and Moisey Uretsky, had each worked for 10–20 years in the big data and hosting sector before venturing out on their own, allowing them both to have the right skills to launch a venture but also to see issues and easily spot problems with the existing competitions offerings.

Exercise: Make a rank bank

Either on your own, in your team or with interesting and interested friends, cut A4 sheets of paper into eight equal pieces and each write one thing on as many pieces you can that you're really good at. These can be specific, e.g. Work things, like designing user interfaces or editing copy, or more personal things like playing the guitar to vague skills like filing. Swap your pile of papers with someone else and get them to rank yours from what they think you really are amazing at to less so. On a table form these into a grid with a column for each person and with 'best' to 'worse' running vertically. See what the top two bands tell you, discuss and move around. Use the final top line to try and come up with, however crazy, business ideas that would make the most of these skills. To help, you could try and fit existing businesses to your skill sets. A slight tweak to this is for the participants to write down and rank what your company is really good at.

No. 2: I Want One of Those

As highlighted by my Dropbox story, many of us go through life often thinking, 'I wish there was something to ...', 'Why hasn't someone made this?' or 'This is OK, but would be better if ...' but generally move on and forget those little sparks often born out of personal frustration.

In 2011, Kimberly Bryant, frustrated by her daughter's experience at a coding camp that was somewhat unintentionally, although unfortunately, gender and race biased in its cohort and teaching staff, bet her pension pot on founding Black Girls CODE, with little or no knowledge of the sector. Bryant has now seen her daughter Kai enroll in a Computer Science degree and Black Girls CODE is now on a fast-track mission to train 1,000,000 more like Kai by 2040.

Exercise: Mindful consuming

This is a kind of mindful exercise. Think of yourself as a business poet, looking for inspiration in the world around you. Pack a small notebook and pen in your pocket. Spend a day just pausing as you pick up things at home and at work, go to shops, cafés, drive your car, ride your bike. Question what ends up in your hand – does it work well, look good, how would you like to change it? This isn't supposed to be a search for an actual idea (although you never know what you'll come up with), but to get your mind into a questioning state of the products and services you consume and that surround you.

No. 3: It's Never About the Money

Forget how successful an idea might be, the market size or the millions you might make from some future stock market listing (IPO) and focus your thoughts on what you really like doing, what you get totally absorbed in. Those activities that eat the hours and mean you forget to eat, or even the ones you've never tried but dream about doing. Some people find it useful to reflect on their childhood selves and often identify long-forgotten, or side-lined, passions. Research (Cardon et al., 2009[*]) shows that passionate founders tend

*Cardon, M.S., Drnovsek, M., Singh, J., Wincent, J. (2009). 'The Nature and Experience of Entrepreneurial Passion.' *Academy of Management Review*, Vol.34, No.3.

to be more creative, persistent and successful than those coldly following the money. Passion is often the perfect fuel for entrepreneurial success.

Self-confessed reluctant businessman Yvon Chouinard spent his twenties sleeping in the wild, avoiding park rangers and seeking out rocks and mountains to climb with his buddies. His passion for climbing led him to travel the world and eventually forge his own climbing equipment and start to sell outdoor clothing to get by. From this, outdoor activist of a company, Patagonia, was born, with all of Chouinard's passion for the outdoors and our planet baked in. The result is a business with $1n in annual revenues. Despite this, Chouinard says, 'I've been a businessman for almost 60 years. It's as difficult for me to say those words as it is for someone to admit being an alcoholic or a lawyer' – and would still rather be seeking out an unclimbed mountain to scale or going off on his own to fish all day.

Exercise: Time to time travel

It's time to wind the clock back. Remember your school days. Focus on the lessons, activities and pastimes that you loved, the books you took from the library or family bookshelves, the science kits you got for Christmas – whatever you did to eat up the days in the long summer breaks (especially before technology). Perhaps you still do those things or they've become a hobby, or maybe you don't anymore. Be honest with yourself and consider which of them would just make you happy to do all of the time. Take one of these things and dedicate a solid two hours doing it and doing it solely – you might want to find the right space and place to do it and turn off and away from distractions. When you're done, spend some time researching or simply brainstorming any business ideas around your passion that come to mind.

No. 4: Ride the Wave

Keep abreast of change – social, economic, technological, political, regulatory – read widely, absorb everything and look for ideas that are now only just possible. You don't have to be the tide pushing the wave and metaphorically driving the change, but you do want to see the big one coming, stand on your board and catch it.

American neuroscientist, author and entrepreneur David Eagleman teaches at Stanford University but is also CEO and co-founder of Neosensory, a company that develops devices for sensory substitution and chief science officer and co-founder of BrainCheck, a digital cognitive health platform used in medical practices and health systems. In a recent radio interview, Eagleman talked of his postdoctoral time studying for a year at the Salk Institute for Biological Studies in San Diego under the auspicious tutelage of one Francis Crick, one of Britain's great scientists, best known for his work with James Watson, which led to the identification of the structure of DNA in 1953. Eagleman says, 'Every time I walked into his office he had a stack of journals, Science, Nature *and so on, and he would just be flipping through them. When I asked him what he was looking for, he said, "I don't know." Crick simply read and absorbed everything coming out and thought big ideas as a result.'*

Exercise: Look to the horizon

Let's try and channel our inner Crick – even if the ideas we generate are more modest and perhaps not Nobel Prize worthy, they may have merit. Once a month, go out and buy or collect a stack of (real or virtual) journals, newspapers and magazines that just interest you. It doesn't matter what. Now set aside an undisturbed hour and flick through them, read anything that interests you, cut out paragraphs or whole articles and collect them together in a folder or notebook. That's it. I guarantee you'll end up thinking about some of them, talking with friends about them and ideas will flourish. You could even organize this a bit like a book group with friends and colleagues you like discussing things with – each of you have to bring something, anything, interesting you've read, present it for two minutes to the group and then allow five minutes for group conversation, questioning, etc.

No. 5: Slightly Better Cards

Unlike 007 at Monte Carlo, nonchalantly laying down a Royal Flush to bankrupt his arch-enemy, most games of poker are won with a relatively lowly two pairs. In fact, 58 per cent of all poker hands are won with a pair or two pairs. James Bond's signature Royal Flush actually accounts for less than 1 per cent of poker hand wins. To win big at poker, a full house or royal flush can be a killer, but all you really need are slightly better cards than everyone else at the table; the same can be said of a lot of highly successful ventures. Studying what other successful ventures do and looking for variants and improvements to their products, services or models can be a great source of innovative ideas. You may not end up competing directly with the companies you study but off-shoot ideas and new ventures might still be generated.

Who would decide to take on Amazon and compete with what is surely the most advanced fulfilment organization ever created? Seems crazy, doesn't it? Well, not for Martin Bysh and Paul Dodd. As Bysh recently put it, 'Paul and I were poking around in e-commerce, looking for something to do together. I was bored, running a market research SaaS company I'd founded and since sold while Paul was working in global logistics technology for P&G.' Their venture, Huboo, was born while chatting on the touchline of a football pitch and in a few short years has raised over $100m from the likes of serious investors such as Mubadala Capital, Stride, Ada Ventures, Hearst Ventures, Episode 1 and Maersk Growth, grown rapidly to employ over 500 staff and now expanding into Europe and expecting a $1.5bn valuation at their next raise.

Huboo is a full stack fulfilment partner, offering an end to end service for small and start-up online retailers and ecommerce sites. By building a complete software platform, buying and developing state-of-the-art warehouses and offering a hands-on account management approach, Huboo lets their clients get on with sourcing, making and marketing their products without having to worry about anything logistical. Their original 'marginal gain' was a great product market fit with these smaller retailers through the use of modular micro hubs within their warehouse, which enable *staff to pick and pack highly variable items and order smartly and efficiently. Unlike Amazon, their system isn't focused on transiting huge volumes of the most popular items and, as a result, is highly appealing to small, specialist retailers. And the model is appealing to investors too as it is both highly scalable and capital-light, as warehouses can be launched within weeks.*

Exercise: The search for marginal gains

One tried and tested way to start thinking about this approach to innovation is through the concept of marginal gains first made famous in the sporting arena. After years of mediocre performances and few wins, Dave Brailsford used this approach with the British Cycling team, leading them to win 60 per cent of all gold medals in the 2008 Beijing Olympics. He said afterwards, 'The whole principle came from the idea that if you broke down everything you could think of that goes into riding a bike, and then improve it by 1 per cent, you will get a significant increase when you put them all together.' A simple activity here is to look at a range of competitive products or services in your chosen market sector and simply make a long list of the ways they could be 1 per cent better. Not 50 per cent better, not even 10 per cent better, but each statement you write should be hyper marginal – see how many you can come up with.

No. 6: The Wisdom of the (Carefully Selected) Crowd

'The masses are always wrong,' said German poet Charles Bukowski. Perhaps he's right and that broad-based market research is flawed. However, talking with selected groups, especially other founders or investors about problems they're facing, can lead to inspiration. This is really a call to embrace networking, mentors, advisors and to discuss your ideas with them individually. The wisdom of the random masses may be wrong, but a mass of qualified wisdom from people you trust, like and admire may uncover gems of potential innovation. In some ways this is simply the art of research as opposed to market research. That said, crowdfunding platforms play a role here too; whether the crowd on any given platform is carefully selected might be questioned, but they are at least self-selected investors or venturers who can perhaps see something en masse that might not be apparent to you or me.

When three friends got together and decided to make a card game and put it on Kickstarter, the leading crowdfunding platform for creative ventures, they viewed it as a bit of fun and thought perhaps they'd raise $10,000, make a few sets and maybe a buck or two. Instead, when their Exploding Kittens proposition went live it rapidly pulled in $8.8m and the friends, Elan Lee, Shane Small and Matthew Inman, *were suddenly faced with having to produce and distribute over 700,000 packs of cards. The venture was profitable within months, they were getting calls from Hollywood studios for spin-out shows and regular acquisition offers all stirred Lee, a serial founder, to reflect, 'It's the most exciting and terrifying new company I've ever started.'*

Exercise: Connections versus the crowd

So you've got an idea? Try this simple A/B version of a test for it. Devise whatever questions you would normally use to test it out or to get some market research and run this as usual past a selection of your actual or potential target customer base. Alongside this, carefully select 20 trusted contacts on LinkedIn (ideally, not colleagues, friends or family) and ask them the same questions via a direct message. Now compare the differences and similarities.

No. 7: Check the Trash

Some things are just broken and need to be innovated. This is a take on the old adage that 'necessity is the mother of invention', but slightly twisted to be a pro-active hunt for broken products, services and industries to see how they might be fixed.

There are lots of disruptive ventures out there, but perhaps the king of disruption is Wikipedia. It wasn't built on any previous digital iterations but almost instantly usurped the incumbent, centuries-old, market leading printed encyclopaedias. As Wikipedia pages grew and grew, Encyclopaedia Britannica's revenues fell and fell from a high of $650m in 1990, eventually forcing them to print their final volume in 2012.

Exercise: Finding broken things

Look around your office, your home, kitchen, study or store and select five seemingly traditional items – anything that hasn't changed in decades – a saucepan, for example. Get on Google and do a search for any modern innovations in the product, whether technical or in terms of production or business models. If you're struggling to find anything, what's the conclusion? Is the product just the best it can be? Or, having done this, have you started to think of any way it could be better? Really the last big innovation in saucepan technology was the invention, by accident, of the non-stick coating Teflon, back in 1938. Recently, a few companies – chiefly, Simr – have been attempting to integrate smart technologies into this most basic of kitchen equipment. If they're eventually successful in getting us to accept and buy their products, it will be a huge leap forward in this market.

Opportunities are subtle

Don't expect to instantly come up with some new groundbreaking innovation or venture through some of these exercises and thought experiments, although that would be nice. The point is to give our minds and imaginations a sort of innovation workout and through this, attempt to spot the subtle opportunities that may germinate through doing them.

Spotting and acting on these subtle opportunities is then key on the journey to entrepreneurial success. As discussed earlier, the character traits often associated with successful founders and innovators often include grit or resilience, but these alone are unlikely to lead to new ideas and the founders rich in them are rarely simply determined opportunists but often also pattern seekers who can spot these subtleties and act on them. To do so, they have to have a sense of creativity. Perhaps think of these founders as endurance athletes, running an ultra-marathon through some mountains. They are determined to succeed, have the resilience to keep going, but still notice the wild orchid by the path, the cloud shaped like a leaping dolphin or the incongruous industrial building in the distance.

Being able to see patterns, and especially ones out of context and not entirely obvious, is an important element for generating creativity. Fashion designer Paul Smith once said, 'Inspiration comes from observation. I get inspiration from seeing things that are out of context. It could be a Ferrari parked outside a fourteenth-century monastery. The fact that they clash with each other could be the inspiration for combining a denim shirt with a cashmere suit or putting a modern chair in a traditional environment.' Being able to view the world, your environment, product, service, idea or competition through a lens of abstraction like this is key to getting your imagination fizzing and to imagining new futures.

Imagining these futures is a key to successful entrepreneurship and the study of this phenomenon has become a cornerstone of academic work and research around how individuals, ventures and organizations can generate radical innovation. By forming these imagined futures, existing and nascent ventures are allowed to explore a wide range of potential scenarios – competitive activity and risk, crucial relationships and product development options, for example. However, much of the research in this area has focused on the mechanistic elements of these processes such as prototyping, modelling, use of templates, business canvasses, but has infrequently looked at the real actors and agents in all this and the specific roles, vision and skills they bring, i.e. the entrepreneurs themselves – and, perhaps more importantly, how they use and apply these tools at their disposal to create useful imaged futures that might potentially become valuable real futures.

In a fast-changing world embroiled, seemingly constantly, in various short- and long-term crises, successful entrepreneurs and innovators are the ones who will help us all, not just to adapt to these new challenges and environments, but to thrive in them and develop their imagined futures into our real futures. Resilience is all well and good as a survival trait in the short run, but relevance, or perhaps even re-invention, is key to long-term change. Preparing for an article for the *Harvard Business Review*, Martin Reeves and Jack Fuller*, interviewed 250 companies to understand the changes they were making in light of the 2020 COVID crisis. Almost all had reacted and changed practices as a result of the crisis whereas very few had considered re-imagining their potential futures – those who do are the most likely to thrive.

Five Walks That Changed My Thinking
2. Tryfan, Gwynedd, Wales, 1985 and 1987

Looking up from Llyn Ogwen in Snowdonia, the triple fin-like peaks of Tryfan are imposing enough. After a tough scramble to the top, you actually find two summit pillars, 'Adam and Eve' to us English speakers, or 'Sion and Sian' in the Welsh tongue, which offer for some an irresistible, albeit terrifying, chance to leap from one to other and gain the 'freedom of Tryfan'. My 15-year-old self, racked with

*https://hbr.org/2020/04/we-need-imagination-now-more-than-ever

vertigo, on a first trip with my school mountaineering club, not just couldn't make the leap, but couldn't even make the summit and backtracked down from the gully below, much to the loosely veiled disappointment of Mr. Kemplay, my Biology teacher.

That night over a youth hostel dinner, I heard tell from schoolmates of the elation and horror of making the jump. I wasn't experiencing FOMO, but perhaps HAHMO – horror at having missed out. Over the following years, through a concerted effort of embarking on numerous mountain walking and scrambling trips, I all but cured my vertigo and eventually made my return to Tryfan. Through some willed disassociation of reality, eyes closed (not recommended), the leap was made. That feeling of overcoming something through sheer will has stayed with me ever since and drawn me to the outdoors and to adventure whenever my mind is troubled or I need to clear and sort my thoughts.

CHAPTER THREE

Breakout of the Bored'room

'If you had to identify, in one word, the reason why the human race has not achieved, and never will achieve, its full potential, that word would be "meetings".'

Dave Berry

Homo Sapiens have been around for about 300,000 years, give or take, and have pretty much spent all of that time not in the office or in meetings. If you take the industrial revolution as a turning point in this behaviour, then humankind has spent 99.91 per cent of its collective time on the planet not in meetings. And if you take the technological revolution of the late 1980s as your benchmark, this rises to 99.98 per cent. No wonder it's not a natural place for us to do anything and certainly not an environment in which we could hope to reach full potential.

The supervisor of my aborted (possibly postponed) PhD exploring the entrepreneurial drivers of the Iron Age maritime expansion of the Phoenicians into the Western Mediterranean, Dimo Dimov, Professor of Entrepreneurship and Innovation at the University of Bath, thinks deeply about this stuff. Through his academic and practical work on what he and his colleagues call 'Kinetic Thinking', Dimov has proposed that most modern management structures are historically, and somewhat inadvertently, designed to put up structural 'fences', which both stifle individual and team imagination and inhibit valuable serendipity, both of which should be key to developing new ideas and driving innovation. Locked within these established, widely accepted and frequently taught structures, managers and sometimes founders strive to 'know before doing' and rarely 'do before knowing'. As a result, their ability to take metaphorical Indiana Jones-style leaps of faith becomes tightly constrained as they strive to measure, test and see what will support them across the conceptual abyss.

In these contexts, the somewhat ubiquitous sequential meeting and 'business model canvas' driven approach to venture planning runs the risk of forcing founders to focus on some future end-shape of their proposed business or innovation without defining much strategy in terms of how to actually get there and may often introduce risky or un-thought-through assumptions into the process. The key issue, especially in early-stage venture or innovation processes, is that we dive too early into structural issues, customer tests, profit and loss, with cost structures leading us to unintentionally start building some of Dimov's 'fences' from the outset. As Marty Neumeier says in his book, *The Brand Gap: How to Bridge the Distance between*

Business Strategy and Design[*], 'Even back in the command-and-control days of the production line, Henry Ford's decision to manufacture automobiles was driven by intuition rather than market research. "If we had asked the public what they wanted," he explained, "they would have said, 'faster horses.'"'

A 2021 paper, *Imagining Futures: Theorizing the Practical Knowledge of Future-making*, from Neil Aaron Thompson and Orla Byrne[†] delves more deeply into the role of intuition or, as it may be better put, the concept of future-making. This is not solely based on what past, existing data and information is at hand, stating, 'The study of future-making has recently gained prominence due to a growing recognition that imagined futures are a cornerstone for understanding the temporal dynamics of organization, strategy and entrepreneurship. As the future is unknowable, entrepreneurs, managers and workers cannot act solely by identifying optimal choices based on past statistical information (rationalism) or using explicit scripts, rules and norms (institutionalism). Instead, they create and use imagined futures to attend to questions of possibility.'

Generating imagined futures, or novel or wild ideas, is key to successful innovation and requires techniques of openness and play, much more than any traditional formal structures or

---

[*]Neumeier, M. (2005). *The Brand Gap*. New Riders.
[†]Thompson NA, Byrne O. *Imagining Futures: Theorizing the Practical Knowledge of Future-making*. *Organization Studies*. (2022); 43(2):247–68.

employment of some sort of pure reasoning. Before gathering a team together, engaging some advisors or facilitators and diving into another business canvas session in a soulless meeting room, founders and innovators should be concentrating on increasing pure creativity and idea generation. Perhaps only then will the canvas and sitting around a meeting table become truly useful tools to interrogate them – a sort of running them through the mill process – where most new ideas could – and should – be rejected. But how and where should these pre-canvas creative sessions take place?

The Never Bored'room

In a local co-working space I have used on and off over the years, they have a room called the 'Never Bored'room'. It's airy, funkily furnished and decorated, and quite a nice place to meet if you have to. But shouldn't the bar for our meetings be set slightly higher than simply not being bored? Is the meeting, seminar or boardroom a place for coming up with new strategy, free thinking, innovation or perhaps even training to take place? As the late Ken Robinson said in his seminal book on learning to be creative, *Out of Our Minds: The Power of Being Creative*[*], 'If you ever lose consciousness and wake up wondering where you are, check whether you

*Robinson, K. (2017). *Out of Our Minds: The Power of Being Creative*. Capstone.

have a thick marker pen in your hand and a large sheet of paper in front of you. If so, there is a good chance you're on a management course.' Even if we haven't actually dozed off in a meeting, most of us can relate to Robinson's key point. Of course, some training and development is exceptional, creative and inspiring, but more often than not, we're thrown together in a soulless room for a day or half a day in the blind hope that we find some inspiration.

Perhaps central to this has been the ubiquity of brainstorming as a central management and training technique, ever since Alex Osborn devised it back in the 1930s. Advertising executive Osborn proposed the technique and coined the phrase in his 1942 book *How to Think Up* specifically for the purpose of product development, but since then it seems to have pervaded all areas of business and even our schools, colleges and other education setting. By design and on paper, the technique seems to be aimed at developing new and creative ideas, especially if done as Osborn intended, utilizing his four rules:

1) There should be no initial judgement, analysis or criticism of the ideas proposed;
2) Freewheeling is to be encouraged, however strange or left field an idea might be;
3) As many ideas as possible should be generated;
4) Ideas should be combined, or 'piggybacked' to potentially generate even more ideas.

Osborn claimed his technique could increase creative performance by a full 50 per cent. This all sounds good, seems intuitively right, and we've probably all been in rooms covered in Post-it notes full of *new* ideas. But the real truth is that we've been kidding ourselves and have been fooled by a multitude of management trainers, as it turns out that brainstorming does not actually produce ideas that challenge any prevailing paradigm and tends in practice to lead to paradigm-preserving ideas, not new ones. And we've known this for a long time through research, and perhaps simply in the back of our minds.

In the mid-1990s, at the height of the internet bubble, when in their words, 'Radical and discontinuous change is the order of the day', academics, Murli Nagasundaram, a leader in design and creative thinking and then Associate Professor at Boise State University, and Robert (Bob) Bostrom, Professor at the University of Georgia, tested brainstorming techniques*. They found that the free association process embedded in brainstorming and specifically the piggybacking approach of Osborn actually and actively limit the participants' use of imagination to develop new ideas. We certainly are now living in times of increased radical and discontinuous change again and yet, 30-plus years on, we

*Bostrom, R., Nagasundaram, M. (1994). 'The Structuring of Creative Processes Using GSS: A Framework for Research.' *Journal of Management Information Systems*. Vol 11:3.

have not widely changed our approaches in this area and often revert to brainstorming for inspiration.

Brainstorming just doesn't work

In 2010, deciding to investigate Nagasundaram and Bostrom's findings more deeply, Brian Mullen and his colleagues studied over 800 business teams and came to the quantitative conclusion that brainstorming groups were actually significantly less productive, both in the quality and quantity of original idea generation, and in fact individuals were more likely to generate original ideas when actively *not* interacting with each other. To some degree they weren't particularly surprised, as their findings were highly consistent with the predictions they'd already made based on social psychology theories. And this really shouldn't come as a surprise to any of us given the relatively obvious limitations embedded in brainstorming activities, including:

- **The bystander effect:** Simply put, people are less likely to participate, or help, if others are present. This social psychological theory came about after the 1964 murder of Kitty Genovese, stabbed outside her apartment building in New York as 38 witnesses saw or heard the attack but failed to call the police or come to Kitty's aid. More recently, a 2019 study (Hussain et al[*])

*Hussain, Insiya; Shu, Rui; Tangirala, Subrahmaniam; Ekkirala, Srinivas (2019). 'The Voice Bystander Effect: How Information Redundancy Inhibits Employee Voice.' *Academy of Management Journal*. 62.

showed that this effect is also prevalent in workplace settings and leads to subordinates refraining from raising alternate opinions or ideas with their managers.

- **Evaluation apprehension:** Some people, especially introverts and less confident individuals, will worry more about the other participants' or the facilitators' views of their ideas and hence end up contributing less and less if more experienced, outspoken colleagues are present in meetings. Originally proposed by Psychologist Nickolas Cotterel in 1972[*], Milton J. Rosenberg, prominent social psychologist and Professor of psychology at the University of Chicago, later defined[†] this as 'an active, anxiety-toned concern that he [the subject] win a positive evaluation from the experimenter, or at least that he provide no grounds for a negative one.' Simply put, confident people tend to aim for positive evaluations and less confident ones refrain to avoid negative ones.
- **Reversion to mediocrity:** Generally, a group's performance will tend towards the mean or average. This is a well-known phenomenon in sports, where elite athletes take care to limit training with those less competent as it has been shown to reduce their own performance. In group discussions, and especially brainstorming, the gathering and clustering of ideas tends to yield

[*]Cottrell, N.B. (1972). Social Facilitation. In C. McClintock (ed.), *Experimental Social Psychology* (pp. 185–236). New York: Holt, Rinehart & Winston.
[†]Rosenberg, Milton J. (1965). 'When dissonance fails: On eliminating evaluation apprehension from attitude measurement.' *Journal of Personality and Social Psychology*. 1 (1): 28–42.

results closest to some common denominator with potentially key insights or new ideas being overlooked or ignored.

- **Confirmation boss bias:** Somewhat subliminally, there will be a tendency to find, articulate and support solutions that a team thinks their managers or bosses believe or want to hear. Or, perhaps more dangerously, if a CEO or senior manager proposes their great new idea or concept and directs their team to research, conduct feasibility and comment on it, it is much more likely to be agreed upon and adopted regardless of any absolute value or originality.

With all this potentially going on in any brainstorming session, it's no wonder that they are rarely the forum for innovation, even if you don't doze off. Yet, given these accepted and tested creativity limiting effects, and many people's direct experiences, brainstorming is still the most-used management technique for idea generation. For years we've known that brainstorming doesn't work and yet it seems we can't resist the draw of it, to gather our teams together, grab our Post-its and markers and sit around a table hoping to come up with *new* ideas. And, almost all of us are guilty of it – I am definitely a recovering brainstormer. But I resist! Richest person in the world and perhaps most famous entrepreneur of his generation, Elon Musk is famous for simply getting up and leaving meetings if he feels he's not adding to them, or is getting nothing out of them. But let's take a step back and question whether we need that meeting in the first place.

Brainstorming then seems to be more of a management placebo than any powerful technique for generating innovation. I doubt anyone is ever reprimanded or perhaps even questioned about why they're scheduling another team brainstorm session, but perhaps they should be. It is definitely time to ditch Osborn's work – 90 years of unproductive creative meetings is simply enough.

Glenn Gaudette of Boston College put this very succinctly – 'brainstorming is dead'. He talks eloquently about his thoughts on creativity being central to innovation and innovation being central to entrepreneurship, and for him and a growing army of researchers and innovators, brainstorming is simply not the mechanism to generate any of this.

Challenging paradigms

Being creative and generating new ideas or strategy is all about challenging a prevailing paradigm, be that in product development, venture design, go-to-market planning or probably almost any area of business. What we should really be striving for is more than paradigm exploring or questioning. And, if not as far as paradigm shifting, then at least paradigm stretching techniques if we are to generate real new ideas and drive real, radical, innovation.

Elspeth McFadzean, whose work both in the private sector and as a visiting fellow at Henley Business School promotes creative thinking and facilitative leadership through group work, education and research, studied a wide range of accepted creative problem-solving techniques used in business and organized them on what she calls a 'Creative Continuum'* from those that are paradigm preserving to those that can shift the paradigm and generate radically new ideas. Her work supports the ever-growing body of research that brainstorming and related methods are 'safe' techniques that don't tend to flex participants' imagination and that techniques that produce paradigm shifting results have to involve imagination. The key it turned out to unlocking this paradigm shifting or to properly challenge ideas had to be focused on expressive techniques which were often, and most effectively, generated through those that involved fantasy or unrelated stimuli – something very hard to find or generate in most meeting rooms.

Although all likely during their careers to be guilty of running or participating in some brainstorming sessions themselves, in a 2021 survey I conducted of founders and co-founders of equity-backed, fast-growing, scale-up companies, over 75 per cent of the respondents reported that they had their best idea 'not at work'. When asked

*McFadzean, E. (1998). The Creativity Continuum: Towards a Classification of Creative Problem Solving Techniques. *Creativity and Innovation Management*, 7(3), pp.131–9.

where they did have their best ideas, the top five results were:

Outdoors	95 per cent
Holidaying	78 per cent
Working	78 per cent
Exercising	72 per cent
Reading	62 per cent

Counterintuitively to this, it seems that although the majority didn't have their best ideas *at work*, they did have good ideas when doing something they identified as *working*. And in fact, a third of the respondents then cited *working* as the biggest inhibitor to having enough thinking time. At first glance it seemed complicated to unravel these seemingly contradictory findings, but having followed up with numerous respondents the key issue seems to be centred on where the *work* happens and a strong sense that work generally falls into two discrete areas which I label the 'to-do list' and the 'to-think list'. Whatever tool, notepad, app you use to plan your work, splitting your tasks into these two distinct groups is powerful in itself – i.e. just making the lists makes a difference to your thinking. Use meetings for the to-do list but question whether a meeting is any good at all for the items on your to-think list. As I discovered from my survey of founders, deep, cognitive, creative work doesn't stop at 5 p.m., but it is good practice to leave your work to-do list at the office.

Bunking off is good

Many years ago, I was in New York talking to a senior Googler about Eric Schmidt's 70:20:10 rule, at the time groundbreaking, where 10 per cent or half a working day of his and Google employees' time could be spent on projects that were completely unrelated to their core roles. Adapted for a business environment from an established theory of learning, the core idea was that 10 per cent of time was when 'disruptive innovation', which might lead to potentially transformational projects, could and would be generated. Schmidt believed that the key to innovating or inventing things for markets that don't even exist yet was creativity and a key tenet of this policy was that working on areas outside of your core expertise could generate these 'sideways' ideas. *Harvard Business Review*'s analysis of the 70:20:10 rule seemed to back this up, finding that companies that have employed it generally outperformed competitors and produced higher-price/earning ratios driven by successful and sustainable innovation processes.

However, when I asked my Google friend, 'What do you do with your 10 per cent?', he replied, 'Oh, I go home early on a Friday like everyone else.' It turns out he took this time for leisure. At the time I saw this as a sign that Schmidt's rule didn't work very well and for many had become simply an excuse for bunking off early. Over the proceeding years, as a founder, researching and working in innovation, and in the outdoors, I've concluded that he was on to something deeper – that just taking a break from the norm, from his office, to-do lists and meeting schedules was much more likely to be a catalyst for idea generation. Our human brains and bodies simply do not work optimally sat at desks and boardroom tables 9–5, five days a week, 48 weeks of the year.

Michael di Paula, a UK-based pioneer and thought leader in the use of the outdoors in business says, 'In a hundred years or more time, we'll look back at the working practices of this past century and judge them, relatively, in the same way we now view Victorian mills and their cramped, squalid working conditions. Think about it. We've asked people to spend the majority of the week for their entire working lives sitting in one position. Confined to an often uncomfortable chair, hunched over a small desk, peering into a small screen.' I truly hope we don't have to wait 100 years to reflect on this, change things and break these practices.

Some companies are actively experimenting with breaking these patterns of work, albeit often with a central important impetus being an increased focus on employee well-being. In the summer of 2019, Microsoft experimented with a four-day working week as part of their 'Work–Life Choice Challenge'. They closed their offices in Japan every Friday during July and August. The scale of what they observed came a surprise – a whopping 39.9 per cent increase in productivity over the previous year. Less work equalled more productivity, or perhaps less stressed employees equalled more productivity, or maybe, more inspired employees equalled more productivity? Especially relevant to my own thinking, and perhaps difficult to measure the direct effect of in Microsoft's experiment, they also limited meetings to a 30-minute maximum duration and encouraged remote participation and communications wherever required. Plenty of research now backs up the general benefits of a four-day week from the personal – general well-being, stress reduction and work–life balance – to the corporate – productivity, less sick time, reduced carbon footprints and longer average employee tenure. However, the knock-on benefits to employee creativity and innovation have not been looked at closely but are probably significant. Given the results of my research, conversations and surveys, I suspect that through the simple act of having more time out of work, more time to think about other things and much less time in unproductive meetings does actually lead to increased innovation as well as productivity.

Meetings are of course useful and can be productive, so I have no call to kill them off entirely, but simply to analyze them, question them and consider their structure and purpose. Not every meeting is fit for purpose and most become habitual, unwieldy and unproductive. Apple founder Steve Jobs, as well as embracing walking for thinking, had a strict set of rules for his meetings – his Meeting Rule of 3s:

- Firstly, he believed that having fewer people in a meeting was more productive so he kept the invite list to three people (five max). No one should be in the room if they're not actively contributing.
- Secondly, the agenda should be limited to three clearly connected items. If not, it is likely the first rule will be broken and actions hard to determine.
- Lastly, keep the meeting to a 30-minute duration.

Above all, and before a meeting was scheduled, Jobs would ask, 'Do we need this meeting?' Do I actually need the participants' feedback on something? Could an email or phone call work instead? This minimalist meeting culture is appealing but perhaps more suited to very senior executives than to most people's working lives. And are meetings purely functional events? Surely there is a place for them in terms of employee interaction, relationships, conversations to spark ideas and innovation?

We're all wasting our time

Almost no meetings aim for anything like these goals or even Jobs' structure. A 2018 research project by eShare* showed that:

*https://pressreleases.responsesource.com/news/95024/unnecessary-meetings-costing-uk-business-more-than-gbp-bn-a/

- The average office worker spends 10 hours 42 minutes every week preparing for and attending 4.4 meetings, with 2.6 of those deemed to be unnecessary;
- The average meeting was revealed to have 6.8 attendees;
- Seventy per cent of office workers believe there are too many meetings in a working week;
- Twenty-four per cent said that often the same results could be achieved with a few quick emails;
- Seventy-nine per cent of employees say they could get much more work done with fewer inefficient meetings;
- Forty-five per cent believe that meetings prevent them from actually getting on with their jobs.

Added to this pre-pandemic data, aggregated data from Google calendars and the polling of more than 15,000 employees by Reclaim.ai, showed that we now, in our blended virtual and office-based worlds, spend 25.3 per cent more time in meetings: that is, 5.5 meetings per week, 4.5 unnecessary ones eating up perhaps 11 hours, or over a quarter of the average worker's contracted hours.

Taking a broad view on the value and nature of business meetings, in his 2004 book, *Death by Meeting: A Leadership Fable About Solving the Most Painful Problem in Business*, Patrick Lencioni[*] investigates the paradox that although they are often seen as the lifeblood of organizational structure, most

*Lencioni, P. (2004). *Death by Meeting: A Leadership Fable About Solving the Most Painful Problem in Business*. Jossey-Bass.

of us don't actually like meetings and most meetings prove to be unproductive and rarely achieve meaningful resolutions. Postulating that meetings are generally boring and ineffective, he suggests we should aim to inject them with drama and conflict, as well as setting out a methodology around daily check-ins, weekly tactical and monthly strategic get-togethers and a quarterly off-site review. Lencioni suggests that the off-site element should be simple, devoid of distraction and interruption, thus allowing leaders and executives to reflect on the deeper issues and states of their organizations. This is definitely in my 'to-think-about' category. His methodology is all well and good, and has been successfully adopted by many teams and ventures, but perhaps is missing a vital element – that creative thinking and innovation is primarily driven and inspired by distraction, not through the lack of it. We shouldn't try to remove distraction but instead find ways to generate and embrace the right kind of distraction that can actually allow proper reflection and, more importantly, spark creative solutions.

Inspired by distraction

Many years ago, I lived in Pimlico in central London, close to the original Tate Gallery, Tate Britain, on the banks of the Thames. Both child- and relatively care-free, I often wandered aimlessly about its halls at weekends and always ended up transfixed by the 1953 collage 'The Snail' by Henri Matisse that still hangs there today. Something about its scale and abstract simplicity captivated me. It is a hard piece of art to categorize, part-painting, part-sculptural, part-geometric, also figurative, but wholly abstract. Matisse himself perhaps summed it up in his philosophy on art that 'exactitude is not truth'. Leonardo da Vinci, long before Matisse, always tried to view problems from different perspectives on the basis, through experience, that the first way he considered anything was always biased to his ingrained way of seeing things. If we can generate a grain of the creativity of Matisse or da Vinci, then we'll be very happy, I suspect.

Like great art, radical innovation rarely comes from people who are set in their ways, simply know more, or have more information, but from those who manage to generate alternative perspectives. Abstract artists are masters of this technique: imagined from a higher vantage point, the details of a coastline become smeared together, the sand becomes a smooth expanse of brown. At this level of description, different qualities emerge: the shape of the coastline, the height of the dunes, and so on.

Abstraction should also be one of the most basic and powerful principles in restructuring problems in business or searching for innovative solutions. Research backs this up strongly. Elspeth McFadzean, author of *The Creativity Continuum: Towards a Classification of Creative Problem Solving Techniques*[*], suggests that creativity can be enhanced

---

[*]McFadzean, E. (1998). The Creativity Continuum: Towards a Classification of Creative Problem Solving Techniques. *Creativity and Innovation Management*, 7(3), pp.131–9.

by looking at the problem from a variety of perspectives and by breaking old mind patterns and through the formation of new connections and perceptions.

In his 1992 book, *Serious Creativity: Using the Power of Lateral Thinking to Create New Ideas,* Edward de Bono described creativity as moving 'sideways' in order to try different concepts and perceptions. I find the concept of sideways thinking appealing and more useful than lateral thinking as it suggests that we don't have to jump tracks or make leaps of thought, but can find ways to glimpse new ways of thinking out of the corner of our eyes. Too often we focus on the detail of problems and don't take this sideways view of them. Right now, many of us are searching for ways for our ventures to survive, but we should also be looking for ways for them to thrive, to pivot, move sideways and bounce back. Resilience is useful, relevance is key, but innovation is everything.

Let's not kill the meeting then but perhaps think more broadly about them. Some meetings have a purely practical use, some a strategic one, some should have a cultural purpose and some an open, freewheeling creative aim. Most of us have experienced environments where these things happen, just not often at work. At university or college we spend time in 'meetings' where we learn from leaders (lectures), where we discuss our thoughts and ideas (tutorials), where we collaborate (writing groups or laboratory work) or even create (in the studio) and even take time to think for ourselves (research). And the eventual outcome? World-leading research, innovation and new ideas.

I didn't go to art school, but I like the idea and concept, where new ideas come from the simple freedom for exploration and creativity – or what many would call 'play' (perhaps 'serious play'?). Most art foundation courses start with some sort of diagnostic or exploratory phase to help students fully understand their abilities and their interests and to consider wide range of disciplines before any commitment to a particular specialism. Perhaps if more of our meetings were built around the concept of exploration and ideation, then the individuals within our ventures would simply create more interesting ideas, as well as work out their own specialisms and start to spark some real collective creativity as teams and ventures.

Five Walks That Changed My Thinking

3. Poon Hill, Nepal, 1999

You'd hope that after six months of worldwide backpacking and more than a week trekking, away from any twentieth-century technologies, through the foothills of Annapurna in the Himalayas, your mind would be pretty clear. After years of walking, hiking and trekking in the UK and Europe, it was during this trip that I first properly experienced what simply walking, day after day, does to your mind. And it wasn't through struggling up a peak, to bag the summit, or exhausted after a risky scramble, but eventually simply by getting up before dawn and going up Poon Hill. A well-known viewpoint on the trekking circuit, Poon Hill is where Nepalis set up very welcome tea stations while visitors take in the breathtaking sunrise vistas of Dhaulagiri and the unclimbed, forbidden peak of Machhapuchchhre. Thoughts on life and futures simply crystallized here and what was to become a successful venture idea, incubated a month earlier on a Thai beach, was properly born.

The next week spent in isolation recovering from a bout of dysentery wasn't quite such an inspiring experience but hasn't dampened my love of high mountains and the benefits of walking among them.

CHAPTER FOUR

Collective Creativity

'If you want creative workers, give them enough time to play.'

John Cleese

Individual creativity is vital for generating new ideas and coming up with innovative products, services, solutions and for building successful ventures. Those passionate entrepreneurial types among us may feel that they have all of the individual, internal fuel they need to do this. However, even if so, the success, application and development of these ideas generally takes some sort of teamwork – the right colleagues, partners, co-founders, investors, board members and employees – and the collective passion of these team members plays an important part in this success.

In 2017, Linlin Jin of the Guangdong University of Technology and a group of colleagues* made over 8,000

---

*Jin, L., Madison, K., Kraiczy, N., Kellermans, F., Russell Crook, T., Xi, J. (2017). 'Entrepreneurial Team Composition Characteristics and New Venture Performance: A Meta–Analysis.' *Entrepreneurship Theory and Practice*.

observations for their paper analyzing team composition within ventures and found it had significant impact on success. No surprise, I suspect. However passionate and creative the founder or entrepreneur, their ideas often get nowhere without the right team alongside them.

Exploring team attributes further for an article for the *Harvard Business Review*[*] focused on the level of team members' passion for a project. A team led by Managing Partner Eva de Mol at venture capital firm CapitalT found that too much diversity in passion levels within a team was harmful to venture development. What they found was that simply having a mix of team members who were generally passionate but not for the specific project at hand led to decreased short-term team performance, but interestingly that with team members offering passion for different elements of a venture – e.g. those product-orientated people with a passion for inventing, or for the act founding a venture, or for the development phase – also had negative impact in the longer term success. This is the most surprising as it seems really logical to choose a founding team that have diverse talents and passions, but it might not be. We need to be able to both develop collective creativity and passion and recruit for and organize ventures and teams to reflect this. Here, creativity can be both the required process for doing this and the outcome.

[*]https://hbr.org/2019/03/what-makes-a-successful-startup-team

When it comes to early stage companies raising investment, most investors have a strong desire to see a team with more than one founder, whereas others are more relaxed with the solo founder, but all generally like to understand the broader team, their credentials and experience and how they fit together. Why is this so important? Reflecting on their first ten years in business, seed investment firm First Round (investors in Square, Uber, Roblox, to name a few) reported that their portfolio teams with more than one founder outperformed solo founders by a whopping 163 per cent and solo founders' seed valuations were 25 per cent less than teams with more than one founder.

It seems obvious that a successful venture needs to include creative individuals in its founding team but also that those people need to be able to generate collective creativity from the outset and also as they grow and hire. The problem is that this often doesn't happen. In their 2012 paper, 'Collaborative Creativity—Group Creativity and Team Innovation' for the *Handbook of Organisational Creativity*, Mary Dzindolet and colleagues discuss the fact that studies in groups brought together for short-term projects show that they often underperform in creative tasks and that it actually takes

*Dzindolet, M., Kohn, N., Paulus, P. (2012). 'Collaborative Creativity—Group Creativity and Team Innovation'. *Handbook of Organisational Creativity*, 327–57.

considerable training, experience and selection of the right team members to generate successful collaborative creativity. Hoping that by every now and again running some blue-sky thinking or innovation workshops will bring results is a short-sighted and misplaced view. Creative thinking cannot be turned on by flicking a switch or gathering everyone into a conference room, however creative or passionate individually the team members may be.

Organizational Leadership Theorist Olivier Serrat[*] thinks about this kind of thing a lot and has come up with a list of components that a company or venture should build into their DNA if they are to successfully and collectively be creative and innovate:

1) Clarity in mission statements and goals.
2) An organizational culture that values innovation.
3) A systems approach to management that understands innovation as one part of a wider context.
4) The adequate resourcing of innovation in line with strategy.
5) The placing of responsibility for innovation on all staff.
6) Understanding that creativity is desirable but insufficient.
7) An enriched physical workplace that enhances creativity.

*Serrat, O. (2017). *Harnessing Creativity and Innovation in the Workplace. In: Knowledge Solutions.* Springer, Singapore.

8) Human resource systems that ensure staff have diverse thinking (or learning) styles.

9) Team set-ups that avoid groupthink.

10) High levels of decentralization and functional differentiation.

11) Honed knowledge management systems.

12) Numerous and empowered members of relevant communities and networks of practice.

13) Processes and methodologies that identify and share good practice.

14) A performance measurement system that measures the innovative pulse of the organization.

15) The instigation of incentives and rewards for innovative individuals and teams.

16) Plentiful space for creative thinking and reflective practice.

17) Linkages with the marketing function.

18) Effective dissemination systems.

19) Dedicated information systems.

20) Structured intellectual property management systems.

This is an admirable list and perhaps one that all of our ventures can aspire to. However, in small entrepreneurial teams operating or hoping to operate in the fast-moving worlds of a start-up or scale-up, this may all seem too much to take on from the outset. Aspirational yes, but what baby or first steps can we take on a journey to a structure like this?

Give them enough time to play

Running through this list and absolutely key is having the right culture, the right people and plentiful space. By 'space', I mean literal but also temporal – as John Cleese said at the start of this chapter, 'give them enough time to play'. Attitudes to the value of creativity in teams, putting together the right teams and allowing enough time for play can get us on the track to what Serrat proposes. I also suspect that by developing from the outset the right culture and creative mindset and allowing enough time and space for that creativity to flourish, the right people will be attracted.

4.1 The Innovation Culture Cycle

A culture of
creativity

Innovative teams

Real
Innovation

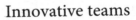

Space and time
for creativity

Not everyone agrees with this. Scientist, inventor and co-founder of the Polaroid Corporation Edwin Land once said, 'There is no such thing as group originality, group creativity or group perspicacity.' I suspect Land was a bit of an outlier, informed mostly through his own scientific methods, which often involved regular, marathon research sessions. The story goes that during these sessions he would brainstorm, think, experiment continuously without a break until he'd found a solution to a problem. Someone would have to remember to bring food and remind him to eat, assistants would work in shifts, being replaced as they became exhausted. Apparently, in one of these sessions he once wore the same clothes for 18 days straight. This could all make for a fine Netflix drama perhaps but is probably not the type of working environment that many of us would choose or would strive to replicate in our own ventures.

Land was working in the mid-twentieth century and time, research and experience has led most people, entrepreneurs and academics to now think very differently about group creativity and how to generate it. That's not to say that it is easy to generate and nurture. Back to John Cleese now, who also suggests that, 'The really good idea is always traceable back quite a long way, often to a not very good idea which sparked off another idea that was only slightly better, which somebody else misunderstood in such a way that they then said something which was really rather interesting.' Can groups or teams effectively spark these initial ideas, germinate and bounce them around, sparking better ones, and are they any good to getting them to Cleese's interesting point?

In their edited volume, *Group Creativity: Innovation Through Collaboration*[*], bringing together research into group creativity, Bernard Nijstad of the University of Amsterdam and Paul Paulus of the University of Texas outline how working in groups doesn't always lead to innovation, highlighting reasons such as:

- Groups may feel pressure to achieve a premature consensus;
- Group contexts can lower accountability;
- Groups that share information tend to focus on common rather than unique ideas.

One of the issues with traditional group ideation techniques is that generally only one person can share their ideas at a time. The issues with this are very similar to those of brainstorming techniques. Nijstad and colleagues offer some ideas – group writing tasks, use of computer-based communication instead of face to face – but also highlight that minority influences in group contexts can increase creative thinking and show the importance of generating and sharing diverse viewpoints.

*Nijstad, A., Paulus, P. (2010). *Group Creativity: Innovation Through Collaboration*. Oxford University Press.

Within a team, and perhaps especially a team, group or venture hoping to innovate, it would be great to be able to harness this process, to build some group creativity or entrepreneurial imaging that encourages diverse and divergent thinking. John Tooby, American anthropologist and co-founder of the Centre of Evolutionary Psychology at the University of California in Santa Barbara, choose to use the word 'coalition' when discussing group problem solving, which I find a useful phrase in itself as for me it stresses the need for multiple voices to be articulated and heard within group contexts. He stresses that as humans, we deeply need to belong to a coalition, which he defines as having, 'propensities to act as a unit, to defend joint interests, and to have shared mental states and other properties of a single human agent'. Tooby and his colleagues use neuroscience techniques to investigate how as humans we co-operate and form these coalitions and how these affect human reasoning.

Collective imagining

The concept of how a coalition could generate innovation brings me back to Chapter 1 (*see also* pages 7–34), where we touched on the research and work of Sara Elias and colleagues*

*Chiles, T., Crawford, B., Elias, S. 'Entrepreneurial Imagining: How a small team of arts entrepreneurs created the world's largest traveling carillon.' *Organisational Studies*, July 2021.

centred on the concept that, 'novel ideas emerge from (un) conscious processes'. This speaks very much to the culture, space and time we require within teams to generate proper innovation. It can't be too forced or 'conscious'. The process model for entrepreneurial imagining they propose is based on five elements: 'experiencing, early creating, reaching an impasse and gestating, (re)creating and evaluating imagined futures, and choosing and enterprising'.

To study and design their model, they followed and investigated a small team of arts entrepreneurs over a 25-month period as they created the world's largest travelling carillon. A carillon is a pitched percussion instrument that is played with a keyboard and consists of at least 23 cast bronze bells in fixed suspension and tuned in chromatic order so that they can be sounded harmoniously together. This may seem a little esoteric or even irrelevant to most people's idea of entrepreneurial activity, but it is the process of team creativity, interaction and imagination that can lead to ideas becoming real that Elias was interested in and her study offers real insight for wider application.

Elias and her colleagues were attempting to offer a practical model for group innovation in entrepreneurial journeys, to embed in this and make clear the importance of imagination to the success of these journeys and to disrupt the traditional, organized approaches most widely used in teams and organizations. Key to this is the acceptance that imagination is where it all begins.

Their model of entrepreneurial imagining, and perhaps any entrepreneurial journey, is by its very nature unpredictable, full of small and big triumphs, setbacks, misadventures and, as Elias says, 'has no beginning or end; it is always in the middle'. Simply by embracing this concept, it becomes rapidly clear that most models and processes used in incubation and acceleration contexts tend to focus on trying to create an A to B journey. But 'play' isn't like this. That's not to say that some processes shouldn't precede or follow others in an innovation process and that it is OK if many aspects are abandoned on the journey – this is OK.

What I like about this model is that within the stages proposed – 'experiencing, early creating, reaching an impasse and gestating, (re)creating and evaluating imagined futures, and choosing and enterprising' – the role imagination plays is key almost all of the way through, right until the moment of choosing and enterprising. This is contrary to most models for innovation processes in that it is designed to lead to, 'improved understanding of how entrepreneurs engage their forward-looking imaginations, which materialize in their everyday performances, to generate novelty and make a difference in the world'. So, imagination or creative thinking comes first and carries on as central to the individuals involved and to how the team explore and develop innovation.

Huboo, who I mentioned earlier in Chapter 2 (*see also* pages 60–1), have been on a rollercoaster of innovation, growth and development in their short history. To grow rapidly to 500+ staff and continue to recruit, open warehouses, develop their platform and launch internationally, founders Martin Bysh and Paul Dodd have had to imagine their own and future ventures from the off and, through this, they have required deep collective creativity to permeate the culture. To grow so rapidly, they had to ensure that staff really loved coming into work, to have fun and play as well as sometimes putting in eight or nine hours of productive time.

Huboo have embraced the trappings of a well-funded, fast-scaling tech venture with the obligatory pool and table tennis table and have added a bar, climbing walls, catering, a games room and even run a work radio station. But it is the deeper commitments that interest me, especially their aim to run the business on the basis of 'minimum viable bureaucracy'. Through this, they aim to truly value the ideas of staff at every level, not just the executive team. Creative ideas for innovation can come from all areas and from all people, suggested through idea boxes, discussed in wider teams, rewarded and celebrated.

This melting pot of ideas feeds into an ever-changing and developing key set of five company-wide ideas that drive innovation and steer Huboo towards an ever-changing imagined future of success. And this aligns perfectly with Sara Elias' proposed stages of '(re)creating and evaluating imagined futures' and 'choosing and enterprising'. By choosing to launch, operate and scale a fulfilment business, it would have been easy for Bysh and Dodd to follow a well-trodden blueprint, but through their innovative model they have been able to harness the individual and collective creativity of their fast-growing staff to achieve both, staying innovative and developing committed and happy people.

As Bysh concluded in a recent interview, 'Huboo is full of people who care passionately about their work and our customers; who want to fix issues without being told to; and who have an inherent ability to always do the right thing. Recently, when a team decided to work late to reach one of its commitments, people from other teams stayed with them to help. This is the level of camaraderie that has evolved at Huboo. We are absolutely committed to our values – integrity, focus, ambition and solidarity. These underpin everything we think, do and say.'

Is playing working?

So should companies take play at work seriously? For many, it may seem a bit frivolous compared to the 'important' tasks of working hard and hitting clear measurable objectives. A large body of research from psychologists has challenged this for some time. Accepted in psychological theory is the concept that play, doing things for no apparent purpose, laughter, joking around, games, socializing and stress relieving help boost our emotional states and allow us to perform better. Specifically, we perform better at experimenting, being creative and are able to generate innovative ideas better when we are allowed to be playful. Allowing teams to explore playfulness should not be considered frivolous, time wasting or even 'nice to do'. The results of playfulness can be of high value, especially when striving for innovation. Some ventures have approached this through their physical work environments – think of the eagerness of tech start-ups to have table tennis tables, computer games rooms and the like – or through off-site team building events. I'm not knocking this, but it is somewhat missing the point that play can be serious, deep work and doesn't only have to address the stress-relieving, light-hearted element of this.

LEGO are serious about play and through their open source LEGO Serious Play methodology believe that creative thinking and team communication can be improved through using their brightly coloured bricks to tell stories and explore ideas. Their facilitated fun-based sessions are designed to help uncover new insights through group participation, often as an add-on or even antidote to longer traditional strategy events.

One case study that appealed to me involved a group of 13 leaders using their session to visualize and create a new mission statement. The facilitator, Derek Good, having led the group through building models and then removing bricks until they had the essence of a good representation of an aspect of trust, reflected, 'I then got them into three groups and showed the mission statement on a big screen and asked them to apply the same thinking. What words could we remove to reduce the length of the statement but still keep the essence of the meaning? After three rounds of discussions, we had it! A new seven-word mission statement (the original was 29 words long) and everyone was on board. In a matter of about 30 minutes, we had achieved something they had taken hours to do previously and now had a succinct message to hang all of their activities on. At the end of the two-day session, the group referred constantly back to the amazing experience of the "chunking" down process that LEGO Serious Play allowed them to experience.'

The participants in this simple approach are free to have fun together, and through building metaphorical models, actually making something and reflecting on their creations together seems to produce results. The problem with approaches such as this perhaps is the very fact that they're brought out, or brought in more often, for a one-off workshop or event and then it's back to the desks for everyone to do some proper work. This doesn't seem to fit well with Serrat's call for organizations to 'create plentiful space for creative thinking and reflective practice'. Organizing the odd creative session with an external facilitator doesn't seem a plentiful approach at all, so how can organizations embed this playfulness more systematically?

Mark Zuckerberg is famous for his mantra 'move fast and break things'. Putting aside recent arguments about the tenability of this approach in light of the perceived abuses of tech companies – as Hemant Taneja of VC giant, General Catalyst, put it, 'In short, the "move fast and break things" era is over. "Minimum viable products" must be replaced by "minimum virtuous products"; new offerings that test for the effect on stakeholders and build in guards against potential harms' – it is still interesting to investigate how this approach actually manifested in the early years of Facebook. Zuckerberg has often told of regular hackathons, where the engineers and large parts of the whole company, would be free to work on and make whatever they wanted, just trying things out, being free to innovate. As an early Facebook engineering lead, Pedram Keyani, recalls, 'In Facebook's early days, a lot of ordinary nights were like hackathons – when someone decided they wanted to stay up all night to build a prototype, they just did it. But as Facebook grew, people started organizing hackathons as a way to collaborate with colleagues from different parts of the team to get their ideas working fast. I had heard a lot about hackathons before I came to Facebook, and about a month after I joined in 2007, I asked another engineer when the next hackathon would be. He just said, "Whenever someone wants to organize it." I immediately went to my desk and emailed the company that I was going to hack the following night and if anyone else wanted to join me, I would get food and drinks. The following night, we had a great hackathon that generated lots of innovative projects and ideas.'

I suspect many of the participants of these hackathons would have described them as fun, not really work at all. And fun can be a very powerful force. In her recent book, *The Power of Fun: Why fun is the key to a happy and healthy life**, Catherine Price defines the most satisfying type of fun, what she calls 'true fun', which comes generally from serendipitous experiences and brings meaningful engagement to our lives. Can we have this type of serendipitous fun at work as well as with our old friends, in teams and groups? Can we accept it as actually being 'work' and harness it to generate innovative ideas? I think we should try. As Olivier Serrat puts it, 'Creativity flourishes in organizations that support open ideas: these organizations create environments that inspire personnel and maintain innovative workplaces; those that fail are large organizations that stifle creativity with rules and provide no slack for change. There is a role for management

---

*Price, C. (2022). *The Power of Fun: Why fun is the key to a happy and healthy life*. Bantam Press.

in the creative process: but it is not to manage it; it is to manage for it.'

Manage for time off, away from normal desk-, computer- or meeting-based work, as this is where innovation really happens. And innovation generated through play and fun has value and can be monetized. Not all of it, of course. It's a bit of a spread bet to be honest, through allowing teams to experiment under the perhaps unstable mix of allowing freedom and having some control. By control, I really mean the space and environment for creativity to flourish. In a paper delivered at the Design Research Societies 2014 conference*, entitled 'Enhancing Collective Creativity through Enactment', Emily Strouse explores the research that shows that groups who move meaningfully, play, pretend or enact produce more creative outputs than those in sedentary brainstorming scenarios. How can we easily introduce meaningful movement, play and fun into our group, team or ventures innovation strategies? Simple: take it outside.

*Strouse, E. (2014) 'Enhancing Collective Creativity with Enactment: A Comparative Study of Design Research Methods,' in Lim, Y., Niedderer, K., Redström, J., Stolterman, E. and Valtonen, A. (eds), *Design's Big Debates – DRS International Conference 2014, 16–19 June*, Umeå, Sweden.

Five Walks That Changed My Thinking
4. Pen y Fan, Powys, Wales, 2009

Given a day or more free, the Brecon Beacons in South Wales, and their highest peak, Pen y Fan, have been my go-to for walking and thinking now for over 20 years. I've walked them alone, with my kids, as a couple and in groups in the baking sunshine, soaked by sideways rain from the Bristol Channel, crawled to the summit in gale force winds and trudged through snow to find a newly crashed, upturned, single prop plane complete with footprints leading away from the open door.

For me, this is a special place in many ways and has helped me clear my mind, filter thoughts, been my 'office', my 'laboratory' and a place to process grief. On one solo trip in 2009, parking up early one morning, I found myself engulfed in thick fog. Knowing the route well, I pressed on and spent the next six hours walking with never more than about 10 metres' visibility. It was like being a moving sensory deprivation tank and was enlightening; it was almost impossible not to focus your thoughts. There was nothing else pulling on my attention, no views, few sounds, almost no people ... It was one of the most relaxing experiences of my life. Our business at the time was hectic, growing but burning cash, there had recently been a new addition to our family and my father had died. I came back from this single day with a clear view of the future: it then took a few years but it did come to pass.

CHAPTER FIVE

Take it Outside – Introducing Outside Thinking

'That nine-to-five is a hamster wheel, man. Get out and break free! Release that fluffy, domesticated hamster somewhere it can truly thrive: the wilderness.'

Jason Hayes in *The New Yorker*,

September 2021

If you've read this far through my book, I hope you'll agree with the idea and proposition that imagination and creativity are key to unlocking entrepreneurial success and innovation, that we all have the potential to do this and that there are plenty of methods, ways and people to help us as individuals and in teams find the keys to unlock this Outside Thinking. To do this, we have to always be mindful of the systemic 'operating systems' we often unconsciously pass our lives working in, surrounded by all sorts of technology and the wrong type of distractions, all conspiring to suppress our imaginations. It is really hard to be creative if all you do is sit at your desk in front of a screen, or spend hours in often fruitless meetings, and try to force out new ideas or some new ways of thinking about problems and innovation.

Although the quote above comes from a very tongue-in-cheek article describing his first wilderness hiking experience, Jason Hayes is right: the wilderness, in nature, outdoors, in forests, woods, by rivers, up hills, in sun, snow, rain or shine, breathing fresh, clean air, alone, with a friend or a group is where Outside Thinking really happens. And it can be properly transformational. The outside is a canvas for creativity that has been with us for millennia.

Even just being outside, breathing clean, fresh air appears to offer huge cognitive benefits. Joseph Allen of Harvard University is a leading researcher, influencer and thinker on the benefits of clean air in office environments and how this can improve employee health and also increase productivity. In one study run by Allen[*], he and his researchers controlled and varied air quality delivered to 24 volunteers over a six-day period. The results were striking. When working in well-ventilated, clean air conditions the participants scored 61–101 per cent higher in the analytical and crisis management tests they were asked to perform. These are somewhat mind-bending results and his research has set Allen off on a mission to change how our office buildings are built and ventilated.

[*]Allen, J.G. (2022). *Healthy Buildings: How Indoor Spaces Can Make You Sick – or Keep You Well.* Harvard University Press.

However great this aspiration to design new workplaces with plentiful clean air, we already have a free, sustainable source of clean air at our disposal and, through accessing and experiencing it regularly, we can all benefit from the cognitive advantages Allen's subjects experienced – clean, fresh air is all around us in nature, outside of our offices – we just need to go out and breathe it in.

Towards the end of his 2005 book, *Nature Cure**, describing his descent, during his early sixties, into and his subsequent recovery from depression, the UK 'father of modern nature literature' Richard Mabey explains that his recovery journey didn't involve any 'submission to the natural world', that his cure wasn't simply through taking a nature pill of some kind and that his repeated attempts to exorcize his depression through repeated exposure to landscape and nature actually left him somewhat disconnected from it. What healed him, he says was 'almost the opposite process, a sense of being taken not out of myself but back in, of nature entering me, firing up the wild bits of my imagination. It was those first stumbling imaginative acts that reconnected me, more than the autumn breeze through the trees.' What was key to his recovery was his imagination, his journeys with lungs full of fresh air and the creative processes he employed using the natural world as his canvas for recovery. Nature or fresh air themselves weren't actually the cure as the title of his book

*Mabey, R. (2005). *The Nature Cure*. Vintage.

suggests, but more akin to the laboratory and chemicals where the cure was discovered. It took experimentation, trial and error for Mabey to find his cure.

Mabey's experience and reflections that the natural world is not simply there as a place to visit, admire, be active in or to make us well resonates strongly with my view that, for all its restorative power, it is the potential of the outdoors as a laboratory or canvas for our own connection and creativity that can bring real change and innovation to our cognitive process and to our creative thinking. I purposefully use the term 'outdoors' as 'nature' seems to be a more loaded term. Pretty much whatever our circumstances, physically, economically and geographically, we can get outdoors in some way. For most of us, our sense of well-being from being outdoors in natural settings tends to be a given and something we acknowledge and that we experience without much actual effort, but we need to actively work in this natural laboratory if we want to get real insight and generate real innovation from being in the outdoors. The outdoors can and should be a powerful tool for our minds as well as our bodies.

Our offices are broken

As discussed earlier in Chapter 3, the modern office environments we tend to work in, coupled with the high levels of technological engagement expected of us and the systemic multitasking asked of us have combined inadvertently to hijack our attention, not raise it. These artificial environments conspire to limit our creativity. Having ever-growing to-do lists and being constantly busy doesn't mean we're getting anything meaningful, or even admirably or efficiently, done. In fact, this 'perfect storm' of distraction directly inhibits our higher-level cognitive functions, our metacognition and our creative problem-solving abilities. Yet these are the very abilities and skills we need to be able to access and nurture to be creative, to be radically innovative and to build exciting new ventures. Given that we're too often immersed in these work environments and work systems – we now spend over seven and a half hours per day using one or more type of media, for example – it is becoming almost impossible to think clearly. How then can we expect to think creatively?

Over recent years, and certainly exacerbated during the COVID crisis of 2020 and 2021, the growing flexibility of our working environments and offices, where work is now carried out in multiple locations – the office, for sure, but also at home, while travelling, in cafés and co-working spaces – has started to blur some of the traditional 'productive' boundaries that existed between home and office, between holiday and work, and has spurred on and allowed researchers and visionary business leaders to explore the outdoors as a place where efficient work could and should be done.

Serial entrepreneur Bart Foster certainly walks this talk through his recently formed Colorado-based venture, Business Outside, which has the goal of 'becoming the standard for leadership and business facilitation for the future of work, which will be hybrid and remote workforces that crave flexibility, but who still need the connection and culture of in-person interactions'. After years sat in the meeting or the boardroom, Foster reflected, 'Teams are stuck "inside" – inside video calls, inside their corporate hierarchy, inside a mountain of email and meetings, and inside their self-imposed limitations on what's possible.' Like me, he is now on a mission to get business people outside – literally and figuratively – and while simply walking in the mountains behind his house in Boulder, Colorado, came to the conclusion that the stuffy corporate cultures and unhealthy meeting behaviours we are so used to and rarely question should have no place in venture building any longer. His experience, gut feeling and inspiration is founded on good science too.

A two-year Swedish interactive study carried out by Charlotte Troije of Malmö University and some colleagues[*] allowed 58 willing participants to explore what office work could be successfully, i.e. productively, conducted outdoors.

[*] Troije, C.P., Jensen, E.L., Stensfors, C., Danielsson, C.B., Hoff, E., Martensson, F., Toivanen, S. (2021). 'Outdoor Office Work – An Interactive Research Project Showing the Way Out.' *Frontiers in Psychology*. 12.

The outcomes were compelling, leading Troije to comment, 'the results showed that a wide range of work activities could be done outdoors, both individually and in collaboration with others. Outdoor work activities were associated with many positive experiences by contributing to a sense of well-being, recovery, autonomy, enhanced cognition, better communication, and social relations.'

The study was focused on what daily working activities could benefit from being done outdoors instead of this being seen as an occasional extra or special event, i.e. 'to understand how such practices can contribute to a more sustainable and innovative working life'. It should come as no surprise that top of the list of practices the participants recorded as being most effectively done outdoors were those that required thinking, planning and creating and were enabled through activities such as the 'walk and talk', outdoor meetings and taking a 'think walk'. From this feedback and data gathered, Troije suggests that we should strive for more integration of outdoor meetings, walks and working outdoors into our organization structures, work schedules and lives as this would lead directly to greater creativity, a more energized workforce and their increased mental agility. Creativity, energy and agility are all essential for increased productivity and innovation, whether in the context of an entrepreneurial start- or scale-up situation or within an established venture.

The knowledge intense and boundaryless character of many of today's working and meeting practices inflicts a high cognitive demand on us all and increases the need for our mental capacities to be in vital working order. High loading of intellectual and intensive work on our minds can directly increase the risk of cognitive stress and associated stress-related mental health conditions. These are commonly characterized by cognitive dysfunction in the domains of executive functions and memory – areas we need most to effectively do a lot of the work we undertake or is expected of us. Hence, it is imperative to explore, develop and for companies to invest in and enable the utilization of workspaces and work habits and practices which support and replenish these cognitive capacities. Only by doing this, can we hope to be continually agile and innovative.

The results of Troije and her colleagues' studies show that enabling habitually office-based workers and employees to incorporate outdoor work into their schedules can directly serve such beneficial purposes, supporting different aspects of cognition, mental health and brain function, and thus supporting a more sustainable and productive work life. Everyone wins here – employees, leaders, ventures and customers – so why don't we all do it?

Time for different conversations

Highly respected facilitator Adam Kahana (including the heady achievement of having received direct praise from

Nelson Mandela) helps people move forward together on their most important and intractable issues and has worked with business and government leaders in more than 50 countries. He believes that simply the act of paired walking and talking is an activity that has profound impact in the work he does. Reflecting on these experiences, Kahana says, 'I've used this paired walk exercise in many multi-stakeholder workshops around the world. It's so simple and yet it's one of the exercises that participants say has the biggest impact on their understanding of their situation and their relationships with others. The walk offers people an opportunity to connect on a human level, as equals and share their perspectives. This experience can produce profound changes.'

And when Kahana uses the word 'profound', he means it. He tells the story of being in Guatemala in the late 1990s, a country devastated through a genocidal war in which the army murdered hundreds of thousands of indigenous peoples. Kahana was there following the signing of a peace treaty in 1996, running a workshop to help key stakeholders practically implement it.

To help break tensions and open up conversations, he asked individuals from both sides to choose a partner and walk and talk for 45 minutes. One pair, Hugo, an oil industry executive, and Otilia, an indigenous human rights campaigner, paired up and set out. Adam tells of how Hugo returned somewhat stunned and reporting that 'Otilia told me a story about her high school graduation that really shook me up. She'd received the highest grades of any graduating student and was given the honour of carrying the national flag on to the stage, but the school wouldn't allow her to wear her traditional ethnic clothing to the ceremony. So, she was forced to choose between having her accomplishment recognized and offending her family and betraying herself. I hadn't grasped how we Guatemalans have built everyday mechanisms for perpetuating the racism and inequality that produced the genocide.'

Hugo, and other participants, simply through walking side by side had managed to have entirely different conversations than those they were having in the hotel meeting room, which produced deeper insight, empathy and real shifts in their perspectives. Kahana has now used this simple technique in his work across the world.

As we've seen, being able to shift perspectives, to spark creativity, creates profound change and generates real innovation. In most traditional meetings, work systems and workplaces this not only practically, but biological challenging. Counterintuitively to finding ourselves trapped under these cognitive and creative constraints, many of us are now employed in job functions or working for ventures that need to be able to consistently rely on us accessing these higher-level cognitive functions for problem solving, for driving innovation and for formulating new ideas. And this need is accelerating rapidly. Creative thinking is becoming a necessity and valuable commodity, given the predicted rise of technological power, IT capabilities, AI and automation. Having reliable access to these cognitive and creative skills will not only drive successful innovation for firms but also career advancement and higher earnings for employees who nurture and demonstrate them.

It has been known and scientifically proven for a long time that exercise boosts the health of our brain, our attention, our thinking and reduces the risk of mental disorders. It is likely this has deep evolutionary reasons related to the enlargement of the human frontal cortex, which has allowed us to mentally 'travel' in time, make collaborative hunting decisions, for example and to formulate new ways of doing things and solve complex problems. This was summed up well by David Raichlen and Gene Alexander[*] when they defined humans as 'cognitively engaged endurance athletes'. If you consider our roots in hunter-gathering groups and the relatively slow process of evolutionary change, this definition makes sense. Physiologically, little has changed since we jogged across the savannah on hunting missions. The sense of embodied cognition tied up in this definition is central to our being human and vitally important. Our human physiology and the

---

*Raichlen, D.A., &, Alexander, G.E. (2017). 'Adaptive Capacity: An Evolutionary Neuroscience Model Linking Exercise, Cognition, and Brain Health.' *Trends in Neuroscience*, Vol. 40(7).

psychology linked to actually moving through space translates directly into our mental sense of progress too. Simply put, we just feel better and our brains work more efficiently when we move. By moving, our brains fizz, we make more connections, see more patterns, become more creative and solve problems on the fly (and we catch more antelope).

Moving towards the future

In her recent book, *Move! The New Science of Body Over Mind*, science journalist Caroline Williams explores and brings together a wide body of research around these phenomena and in some ways, her book is a call to just get out of our chairs and move – the benefits are huge and easy to access for most people. None of us need to give this the 10,000 hours of practice Malcolm Gladwell suggests is vital in his 2008 book *Outliers* to get really good at it, either – it's just moving. Among a host of practical advice to walk, stretch, dance and breathe our way to well-being, Williams stresses the importance of 'going somewhere' as, 'mentally moving forwards through space has been shown in psychological studies to direct thoughts to the future'. Every physical step we take is inevitably into the future, but the path those steps make is entirely in our control, both in reality and in the realm of our imagination. Those paths to

*Williams, C. (2021). *Move!: The New Science of Body over Mind*. Profile Books.

the future may be very personal, but for most of us are also intertwined with our work and often our colleagues' paths.

This intertwining of physical and imagined destinations and the sometimes euphoric climax of completing a walking journey is amplified when walking with others and can be a powerful moment and outcome for teams journeying together. The additional processes of shared storytelling and synchronization within a group or team moving towards these common goals drives this amplification. Such powerful outcomes shouldn't come as a surprise and are somewhat highlighted by the lived experiences of pilgrim walkers. Often following centuries-old routes imbued with a mass of walked, human history, these pilgrimages can also introduce an embodied sense of group walking, even when undertaken as a solo journey. I purposefully don't use the words 'spiritual' or 'religious' as for many this just isn't the reason to embark on those long journeys anymore.

Nature writer, poetic author of fantastic books exploring and reflecting on the power of nature on the human spirit, such as *The Wild Places, The Old Ways* and *Landmarks* and Fellow of Emmanuel College, Cambridge, Robert Macfarlane* believes that most pilgrim walkers are nowadays not generally religiously motivated to take these journeys but that they are

---

*Macfarlane, R. (2012). *The Old Ways: A Journey on Foot*. London, UK: Penguin.

searching for their own meaning through walking. Reflecting in the *Guardian* on researching and writing his book, *The Old Ways*, Macfarlane said, 'Everywhere I went on these journeys, I encountered men and women for whom landscape and walking were vital to life. I met tramps, trespassers, dawdlers, mourners, stravaigers, explorers, cartographers, poets, sculptors, activists, botanists, and pilgrims of many kinds. I discovered that walking is still profoundly and widely alive in the world as a more-than-functional act. I met people who walked in search of beauty, in pursuit of grace or in flight from unhappiness, who followed songlines or ley-lines; I witnessed walking as non-compliance, walking as fierce star-song, walking as elegy or therapy, walking as reconnection or remembrance, and walking to sharpen the self or to forget it entirely.'

Professor Shane O'Mara* set out to study in depth this type of pilgrimage walking by viewing active participants as a sort of 'living laboratory', allowing him to explore human walking as both a socially embedded process and as a biological adaptation. O'Mara says, 'Pilgrim walking is an underexplored human behaviour, found in many cultures across the world, with roots deep in our evolutionary past, likely arising from selection effects on both our

*O'Mara, S. (2021). 'Biopsychosocial Functions of Human Walking and Adherence to Behaviourally Demanding Belief Systems: A Narrative Review.' *Front. Psychol.*, 04 August 2021.

physiometabolic health and on numerous neurocognitive, social and affective processes, collaterally binding us to our groups and their goals.'

As all this suggests, the goal-directed behaviours embodied in walking, whether as an individual or within a group or team, need not be just towards a physical destination: they can be towards an imagined destination (the imagining of which depends on the activity of the hippocampal formation), or even a sought-after psychological state (such as a perception of 'one-ness' with the universe). Many of our work experiences align with this perfectly. We are generally all working in goal-directed environments, whether sales goals, development goals, launch dates, publication dates and although time stamped are all non-physical or imagined 'destinations', we are striving to reach individually or within teams. It is not surprising then that going for a walk is much, much more than just a simple metaphor for these journeys.

The concept of going somewhere frames these walks not as challenges to be overcome, peaks to be bagged, target miles to cover, metres to climb, but as an open space to freewheel, talk and think in. Our conceptual aim should be to move without travelling. It is easy to rush towards a destination when we think about 'travelling', not least as we are generally surrounded by calls to get to places quickly or to take part in races of some kind. Walking for thinking will always get us both somewhere physical and somewhere imaginal. But what 'somewhere' is the right 'where' and how do we get into the right state of mind to 'arrive' there?

Attention restoration theory

Rachel and Stephen Kaplan, professors of Psychology at the University of Michigan and experts in the effects of nature on health, suggest in their paper 'The Restorative Benefits of Nature: Toward an Integrative Framework that Attention Restoration Theory (ART)'* that 'fascinating' natural settings have direct restorative effects, including increasing our attention spans.

We all instinctively know this. After a gruelling workday or when feeling down, strolling around the garden, staring out of a window, or taking a walk instantly improve our states of mind. The Kaplans' work set out to empirically test and measure the idea that natural environments can both rejuvenate us and boost our attention spans. Four cognitive stages we need to travel through to achieve this state of 'restoration' are proposed:

Stage 1: Clearer head, or concentration

In this first stage the aim is simply to let our minds clear of worries, concerns – not through consciously blocking them, but by letting them flow out naturally.

*Kaplan, S (1995). 'The Restorative Benefits of Nature: Toward an Integrative Framework.' *Journal of Environmental Psychology* 15(3):169–82.

Stage 2: Mental fatigue recovery

The second stage allows our ability for directed attention to be restored.

Stage 3: Soft fascination

Using low stimulation techniques or activities offering the all-important element of distraction, the internal noise in our minds is further reduced.

Stage 4: Reflection and restoration

Finally, through immersion in a restorative environment, individuals can properly restore their attention.

In 'Attention Restoration Therapy', these 'restorative environments' require four key components – Being Away – Soft Fascination – Extent – Compatibility. Practically, this means being somewhere you can be psychologically detached from your present mental pressures (Being Away), doing something that gently holds your attention (Soft Fascination), in an environment you feel comfortable being in (Extent), somewhere that brings you enjoyment (Compatibility). Put simply like this, it doesn't seem too difficult to come up with plans and places where we can all experience the benefits of ART, but we might need some help, activities or techniques around the Soft Fascination stage.

In his book, *The Comfort Crisis: Embrace Discomfort to Reclaim Your Wild, Happy, Healthy Self*, Michael Easter suggests that getting into the 'soft fascination' mode through doses of immersion in the wilderness 'is sort of like an extended meditation retreat. Except talking is allowed and there are no gurus. It causes your brain to ride alpha waves, the same waves that increase during meditation or when you lapse into a flow state. They can reset your thinking, boost creativity, tame burnout, and just make you feel better.'

Easter's pragmatic approach appeals to me. There is no Eastern mysticism here, no need to commune with nature, run naked through the forest or hug any trees (although there is nothing wrong with the odd tree hug) and the use of nature isn't some wishy-washy call to daydream our way to new ideas and success. As we investigated in Chapter 2, Brian Barnard (Wits Business School) and Derrick Herbst (University of Reading) recent research[†] showed that to increase entrepreneurial creativity actually requires the employment of some semi-formal processes. Creativity doesn't tend to come from inspired 'flashes', but sustained periods of thought and effort. This was certainly proven right when studied within the

---

[*]Easter, M. (2021). *The Comfort Crisis: Embrace Discomfort to Reclaim Your Wild, Happy, Healthy Self*. Rodale Books.
[†]Barnard, B. & Herbst, D. (2018). Entrepreneurship, Innovation and Creativity: The Creative Process of Entrepreneurs and Innovators.

confines of traditional workplaces and through our common work practices, but does the outdoors actually offer a shortcut to some inspiration? Can the simple fact of being outdoors generate these 'flashes'?

Building on the Kaplans' work, other studies found that even without the structure of ART imposed on people, simple immersion in natural settings also increased performance in other, related, lower-level cognitive function, leading to improvement in tasks such as proofreading. To test whether similar natural immersion and deceleration could have similar benefits to higher-level functions, Ruth Atchley, David Strayer and Paul Atchley of the Universities of Kansas and Utah set out to empirically test if Creative Reasoning skills could be improved simply through walking through nature and in the outdoors.

In their study[*], 56 unrelated and unconnected adult men and women, with an average age of 28, took part in a series of Outward Bound adventures the team had organized for them. Roughly half of them made their way to the US States of Alaska, Colorado or Maine in small groups, where they embarked on four- to six-day guided hikes, during which they were prohibited from using any technological devices. This first group completed a Remote Associates Test (RAT) on the

[*] Atchley R. A., Strayer D. L., Atchley P. (2012). 'Creativity in the Wild: Improving Creative Reasoning through Immersion in Natural Settings.' PLoS ONE 7(12)

morning before they embarked on their hikes. The second half of the cohort completed theirs on day four of their hikes in Alaska, Colorado or Washington.

Developed by Professor Sarnoff Mednick and Martha T. Mednick in the early seventies, RAT is widely accepted as a standard measure of creative thinking and insight-based problem solving. A RAT test involves respondents being used with sets of three unrelated words, e.g. Widow/Bite/Monkey, Cottage/Swiss/Cake or Bald/Screech/Emblem, from which they are tasked with finding another word associated with each of them in some meaningful way. The test is thought to test the parts of the brain that are supposedly the ones generally overtaxed by our modern, sedentary, technological intense working environments. Whether in the pre- or in-hike test groups, the hikers were given unlimited time to independently complete a set of ten RAT items.

And the results? The participants who had spent four days immersed in nature, hiking and disconnected from technology displayed increased performance in creative, problem-solving activities in these tests by a staggering 50 per cent. This compelling study shows the enormous cognitive advantages available to those who take time out in nature and away from their regular work environments and all of the modern distractions within them. In any business context, a 50 per cent increase in 'productivity' or 'efficiency' would have executives and leaders scrambling to implement radical change to their organizations, but why does immersion in nature or hiking in nature have such a profound effect on some cognitive functions? What's going on here?

Getting into default mode

Perhaps it's because these environments put our minds in what scientists term our 'Default Mode'? This Default Mode defines an area of the brain that is most active when we're engaged in restful introspection and can be observed in brain scans when people wakefully rest in MRI scanners and let their minds wander. Mary Helen Immordino-Yang, Joanna A. Christodoulou and Vanessa Singh in their paper 'Rest Is Not Idleness: Implications of the Brain's Default Mode for Human Development and Education'* provide plentiful evidence for the Default Mode leading to increased divergent thinking skills. Ruth Atchley et al† suggest that, given the results of their hiking test subjects, simply the act of walking, in nature, away from technology, effectively engages this Default Mode and offers a sure-fire way of accessing these very divergent thinking

*Immordino-Yang M. H., Christodoulou JA, Singh V. (2012). 'Rest Is Not Idleness: Implications of the Brain's Default Mode for Human Development and Education.' *Perspectives on Psychological Science*: 7(4):352–64
†Atchley R. A., Strayer D. L., Atchley P. (2012). 'Creativity in the Wild: Improving Creative Reasoning through Immersion in Natural Settings.' PLoS ONE 7(12)

skills that are key to seeing new perspectives, formulating new ideas and to being innovative.

Outdoors is good in its own right then, but Marily Oppezzo[*] showed through experimental data that, 'walking, rather than being outdoors, was the driver of novel, high-quality analogies. While research indicates that being outdoors has many cognitive benefits, walking has a very specific benefit— the improvement of creativity.' Across the three studies in her experiments, participants were respectively 81 per cent, 88 per cent and 100 per cent more creative when walking rather than just sitting and resting. I'd encourage everyone to look up her TED Talk on all this and do as Oppezzo says: 'Take Your Ideas for a Walk'.

To understand more deeply the neurological processes behind this phenomenon, Christian Rominger of the University of Graz and some colleagues[†] ran field experiments to test how creativity is linked to bodily movement from a neuroscientific perspective. They identified that simply through moving, we trigger something termed Positive Affectivity (PAA) in our brains. Higher PAA levels leads to more enthusiasm, energy,

[*]Oppezzo, M., Schwartz, D.L. (2014). 'Give Your Ideas Some Legs: The Positive Effect of Walking on Creative Thinking.' *Journal of Experimental Psychology*. Vol 40, No. 4.

[†]Rominger, C., Fink, A., Weber, B., Papousek, I. (2020). 'Everyday bodily movement is associated with creativity independently from active positive affect: a Bayesian mediation analysis approach.' *Scientific Reports* 10(1):11985.

confidence and alertness in us. High PAA levels promote sociability, open-mindedness and our ability to set goals and solve problems so it's no wonder walking has the unique potential to unlock our individual but also collective creativity. Simply put, if we stop moving, we stop thinking well and we'll stop innovating.

This could be because our cognition and some motor functions are intertwined from an evolutionary perspective – that the very act of moving or walking is in some way deeply linked to our thinking. In their paper, 'Thinking, Walking, Talking: Integratory Motor and Cognitive Brain Function'*, Gerry Leisman, Ahmed Moustafa and Tal Shafir show that certain brain regions integrate both motor and cognitive functions and through brain scans, highlighted the immense positive effects on these regions simply through walking. Over the years, plenty of great thinkers, writers, philosophers and artists have experienced and channelled this very effectively, even if they didn't have a clue about the scientific basis of it all. It is in some ways in our collective knowledge and in our nature, it's just that we don't all practice it nearly enough.

Eighteenth-century philosopher Jean-Jacques Rousseau, central influencer of the Enlightenment, French Revolution

*Leisman, G., Moustafa, A.A., Shafir, T. (2016). 'Thinking, Walking, Talking: Integratory Motor and Cognitive Brain Function.' *Frontiers in Public Health.* Vol 4.

and modern political thought, wrote, 'I never do anything but when walking, the countryside is my study.' A radical in many ways, for Rousseau, the thought of sitting and working at a desk was sickening and he claimed only to find inspiration through walking. It was during his long, meandering walks under a summer sun that he found that the pathways he took stirred his imagination, felt his mind sparkling and new ideas forming.

Frederic Gros in his entertaining and profound book, *A Philosophy of Walking**, delves deep into Rousseau's story as well as those of many other great thinkers throughout time and what we start to realize is that this idea of travelling through natural settings as a stimulus for creative thinking has been key to the development of many philosophies, leaps in science and great literature and it comes naturally to all of us. As Gros says, 'By walking, you escape from the very idea of identity, the temptation to be someone, to have a name and a history ... The freedom in walking lies in not being anyone; for the walking body has no history, it is just an eddy in the stream of immemorial life. A long walk allows us to commune with the sublime.'

Gros of course delves into Nietzsche's story too and how he certainly found his 'sublime' when out walking. By the late nineteenth century, Nietzsche was not in very good health at

*Gros, F. (2014). *A Philosophy of Walking*. Verso.

all. In 'Nietzsche: in Illness and in Health'*, William H. Gass reports that Nietzsche had been troubled by ill health most of his life, suffering from haemorrhoids, bad eyesight, fainting fits, sometimes vomited blood and eventually developing severe depression. Recognizing this, he took to the hills and mountains, including the landscapes around the imposing Eiger, in the Splügen Pass and Grindelwald in the Bernese Alps of Switzerland and through the San Bernadino Pass into Northern Italy. Despite his ill health, those months spent in the mountains of the Alps, walking and thinking were to be his most productive period, resulting in some of the century's seminal works on existentialism, ethics and post-modernism.

Take the first step

In a more contemporary vein, Belinda Kirk is a proper explorer, being founder of Explorers Connect, a UK-based, non-profit organization connecting ordinary people to adventurous opportunities. She has walked through Nicaragua, sailed the Atlantic, gained a Guinness World Record for an unsupported row around Britain, pioneered and led youth challenges, expeditions for people with disabilities and conducted scientific research in the Amazon, Sinai and Alaska. If you've ever wanted to join a team kayaking the Northern Passage or

*Gass, W.H. (2012). 'Nietzsche: in Illness and in Health.' *Life Sentences.* Alfred A Knopf.

trekking across a remote desert, Kirk is the one to help you. In her recent book, *The Adventure Revolution*[*], she recalls her inspiring, and sometimes terrifying, tales of adventure but also calls to us to find respite from the pressures of modern work life, the evolutionary mismatch of technologically heavy existences we find ourselves in and explore routes to clear thinking through adventure.

For Kirk, being adventurous is as much a state of mind as a journey or challenge and can enhance our well-being and thinking, however modest and close to home our adventures might be. As she says, 'Before you leave on the adventure, you have a million and one things to do, but as soon as you set foot on the plane, sit on the seat of your bike or turn away from your car with a full backpack, life immediately becomes so much simpler.'

Key to my thinking is that walking and the adventure that comes with it gives you a direction in which to travel, a purpose and hope for the future. These elements are key to our well-being and also mirror important steps in the process to generating successful and even radical innovations.

Apple's Steve Jobs was famous in Palo Alto for going on long meandering, thinking walks. Venture capitalist Marc Andreessen tells an anecdote about driving round his

[*]Kirk, B. (2021). *The Adventure Revolution: The Life-Changing Power of Choosing Challenge*. Piatkus

neighbourhood one day when he had to swerve to avoid what he thought to be a crazy old man wandering the street. On closer inspection, the 'crazy old man' was Steve Jobs, in his trademark glasses and black turtleneck. Jobs also mentioned in interviews that he used these walks for his own problem-solving and creative thinking.

Why is it then that only 17 per cent of adults regularly walk at all, let alone within their jobs and businesses? A short survey I undertook in the summer of 2021 of business leaders would suggest that within a normal working week less than 5 per cent proactively walk, or encourage staff to walk, as part of their business practice. Putting aside the body of science we've already discussed, this simple statistic also seems to go against what many of us naturally experience when walking, what we just feel and know to be right, and highlights that most current working practices and the expectations of employers seem to see it as 'bunking off' in some way.

In recent years, clothing apparel company L.L.Bean ran an experiment by setting up temporary outdoor co-working spaces equipped with desks, WiFi, open-air meeting rooms and (perhaps somewhat importantly) rain covers in locations across New York, Philadelphia, Boston, and Madison, Wisconsin. Anyone and everyone was welcome and could book for free, hour-long sessions to use the spaces. The company had focused on taking actual work outside instead of inviting people on a walk or hike simply as this is what most of us do most of the time: 'We're not viewing this as an escape; the framework is productive time in the outdoors,' said Kathryn Pratt, director of brand engagement at L.L.Bean*.

L.L.Bean are not alone, either. Amazon has built 'Spheres' in Seattle, clear outdoor working spaces based on biophilic design principles. San Francisco-based Campstye has built outdoor co-working spaces inspired by camp grounds, complete with plants, campfires, picnic tables and trailers. Yet, 75 per cent of workers still spend no time outside within their working hours, with 56 per cent reporting that management would perceive their choice to do so negatively. This mindset needs to change and I'd argue that it needs to quickly move beyond the albeit well-meant and somewhat effective transportation of desks and computers outside to something much deeper. To properly accept, embrace and build policy and habits around the outdoors as a canvas and a place for deep work to be done.

Perhaps this is easier in a start-up environment where the rules are there to be broken and you can design an organization from scratch? After working for Facebook and Intel, and a sojourn as an elite triathlete and IRONMAN, Stefan van der Fluit decided his new venture would rip up the big tech rule book, set his colleagues 'free' and allow them to explore their productivity and creativity, where and

*https://blog .doist .com /should -you -be -letting -your -employees -work -outside/

when it suited them best. Bringing together a team of experts across physiology, chemical engineering, microfluidics, miniaturized electronics, machine learning and product design, he is launching FlowBio, who produce an innovative wearable non-invasive patch that captures an athlete's sweat and interprets key bio-markers in real-time, to provide personalized recommendations that allow them to improve their performance.

Van der Fluit describes his venture as a 'sandbox', where there are no desks, no office times and no office, and one that contractually never 'owns' an employee but allows them all to find their own time and headspace to work, innovate and create. Teams and 'squads' at FlowBio flow themselves, form and re-form dependent on the tasks at hand. They act as coaches and trainers to each other. Van der Fluit's own corporate experiences and time outdoors helped him and his co-founder, Giovanni Rovere, design and build this venture model. He tells of the time he spent working in some so-called innovative workplaces, filled with spaces for creativity, nap pods, fully-funded cafés, games rooms and breakout areas, which were more than often empty due to the culture of blind productivity being king.

As van der Fluit says, 'God forbid anyone actually strolling away from their desk to play a bit of PS4 during working hours.' He and his colleagues spent most of their allocated free time in the Starbucks next door hosting their own caffeine-fuelled 'group therapy' sessions before trudging back to their desks and to-do lists. By setting employees properly free, van der Fluit and Rovere have seen rapid increases in innovation, creativity and success at FlowBio, through employees working out, guilt-free, where and when their own deep work happens: where they find their imaginations are sparked and is manifest and, through the acceptance that creativity equals productivity. And, reflecting on where most of their colleagues and employees find this physical and mental space, van der Fluit is clear that it is most often outside, away from their desks.

Introducing Outside Thinking

This all brings us to the conclusion that semi-structured walking-for-thinking, or what I term Outside Thinking, is nothing particularly new, but it's enormously powerful when done at all, even transformational when done 'right' and needs to be solidly embedded in all of our regular working practices.

Someone I have walked with often, and whose team have been somewhat my guinea pigs, Ed Van Rooyen, founder and CEO of UK-based fast-growing tech venture, TCup, sums it up perfectly, 'Myself, my co-founders and some key staff were guided on a short two-day tour, where we explored the best that Wales had to offer. Whilst it never felt like a "work day", our leader carefully navigated our team over the course of two days using the natural landscape to either "broaden our horizons" on the tops of Pen y Fan, where there literally were no boundaries, or he helped us focus on mindfulness techniques when we were enclosed by the Black Mountain Forest. Pure genius and genuinely transformational.' Ed and his team are now 'Outside Thinking 'addicts' and I have the pleasure of leading them regularly.

Outside Thinking can be transformational, but it is not just a matter of turning your commute into a walk, or heading to the hills at the weekend, although these are always to be encouraged and beneficial for your personal thinking. To work properly, there is some semi-formal structure required to get the most benefit out of being immersed in nature, distracted enough to be restored and having our attention steered enough to achieve real transformational thinking.

My friend, Coach and Adventurer Fi Macmillan, defines 'Golden Hours' within her fantastic 'Outdoor Intelligence' framework, where time outside makes us more productive, creative and in touch with our purpose and our intuition. She even has a formula for it:

Nature + Walking = Deep Work + Intuition

The concept of 'Deep Work' here comes from Cal Newport's 2016 book, *Deep Work: Rules for Focused Success in a*

Distracted World', which he defines as 'Professional activity performed in a state of distraction-free concentration that pushes your cognitive capabilities to their limit. These efforts create new value, improve your skill, and are hard to replicate.' Perhaps counter to Newport's call to hide away, build routines, concentrate hard and wear some noise-cancelling headphones to get ourselves into the state where Deep Work happens, it turns out that a highly effective shortcut is simply to go for a walk in nature with the aim of being distracted enough to focus without the distraction of cognitively demanding tasks.

As we explored, ART and the other research findings analyzed in this chapter bring us some hint of what we need to consider in terms of the actual environment or place to walk and think effectively in to raise our creativity, but we should also consider tempo, time span, frequency, solo or group walking and some of the semi-formal techniques that can be used to maximize the benefits, both personal and professional, of Outside Thinking.

Talking tempo

Let's start by talking tempo. As outlined previously, Outside Thinking shouldn't be approached as a challenge to be

*Newport, C. (2016). *Deep Work: Rules for Focused Success in a Distracted World*. Grand Central Publishing.

overcome, a target distance to cover, peaks to be bagged, records to be set, metres to be measured, but as an open space to freewheel, talk and think in. Tempo is key to set your minds into the all-important Alpha or Default State. You need to be open to embrace space, time and movement. Analyzing results from her deep, qualitative study on the experiences of a group of Norwegian academics who practice walking-for-thinking, academic Mia Keinänen*, found that 'there is a specific type of walking-for-thinking that is separate from other types of walking. This walking has an optimal speed that synchronises rhythms of the body with thinking and vice versa.' Keinänen's analysis suggested an ideal, moderate pace of 5–6km/hr readily set the mind to be open to creative thinking and unlocked all of the benefits this brings. One of her participants noted, 'for me there is a sort of maximum speed where I can enjoy the process and absorb. So it mustn't be too fast, then I notice that I get more concentrated on the walking, and the speed, and so, they are obstacles (to thinking).'

It probably comes as no surprise given the physiological and psychological links between walking and thinking that these experimental and lived experiences of the right tempo correspond directly with a person's optimal gait and associated

*Keinänen, M. (2016). 'Taking your mind for a walk: a qualitative investigation of walking and thinking among nine Norwegian academics.' *High Educ* **71**, 593–605.

minimal metabolic energy expenditure. Henry J. 'Bip' Ralston*, whose research during the seventies into the physiology and the mechanics of human walking led to major improvements in artificial limbs for amputees, calculated that this energy expenditure reached its lowest levels at 80m/min, or 4.8km/hr, very much in line with Keinänen's measurement and with the subjective feedback.

Keinänen found that when employing this steady rhythm and speed the participants' walks 'stirred and immersed them in a field of novel perceptions and stimuli'. They reported experiencing new 'perhaps previously unknown, inner perspectives and thoughts'. This is what Outside Thinking is all about – unlocking new ways of thinking, raising our creativity and finally, channelling this into entrepreneurial success and innovation.

On a call with Keinänen, we discussed why she thinks this might be. Aside from tempo, she believes that there is something deeper at work; that movement is key to pretty much all we do as humans and that space, time and movement can be combined to alleviate our cognitive loads really effectively. It is what we're designed and evolved over millennia to do and be good at. Walking and journeys in nature tap both directly and metaphorically into the spatial nature of our memories and

*Ralston, H. J. (1976). 'Energetics of human walking.' In R. M. Herman (Ed.), *Neural control of locomotion* (pp. 77–98). New York: Plenum Press.

any effective decision-making process requires some sort of narrative feedback. This narrative feedback can be channelled beautifully through group discussion outdoors.

This is part of the reason neuroscientist Shane O'Mara* suspects that the prolific writer and thinker Bertrand Russell found that walking was integral to his work. Likewise, the Irish mathematician William Rowan Hamilton, who pondered a single problem on his daily walks for seven years, eventually inventing a number system called quaternions, without which we couldn't make electric toothbrushes or mobile phones.

O'Mara believes that plenty of regular walking unlocks the cognitive powers of the brain like nothing else. His enthusiasm for walking ties in with both of his main interests as a professor of experimental brain research: on stress, depression and anxiety; and learning, memory and cognition: 'It turns out that the brain systems that support learning, memory and cognition are the same ones that are very badly affected by stress and depression,' he says. 'And by a quirk of evolution, these brain systems also support functions such as cognitive mapping,' by which he means our internal GPS systems. But these aren't the only overlaps between movement and mental and cognitive health that neuroscience has identified.

*O'Mara, S. (2019). *In Praise of Walking*. The Bodley Head.

Some years ago, New Zealand-based psychologist Rosie Walford pioneered an outdoor-based creative retreat, the Big Stretch. Each day in the mountains, she would pose an abstract, profound question for the delegates to consider on the day's journey. Walford would lead the group on a long hike or outdoor activity. No phones. No distractions. Open conversation. Just doing little but walking in big scenery. When asked, most of her delegates said they witnessed the most extraordinary phenomenon. Despite not having consciously thought about the question much in the day, in the evening they now came up with deep veins of rich, psychologically revealing insight and creative thinking. And what had produced this new-found profundity? Turns out, not a lot! Just big skies and expansive landscapes allowing their minds to wander.

Walford says, 'Anyone who goes skiing or walking knows how outdoor activities can clear an overstretched mind. There's a reason for that: while you're happily concentrating on being vigorous, the brain slows to alpha state, where your subconscious filters disparate thoughts and resolves the unresolved. This is a mental state where you're more likely to get to the heart of things. After concentrated questioning, alpha is the state of mind where mental incubation occurs. New ideas synthesise, insights pop up, "right" concepts tend to resonate and grow.' In search of innovation and good entrepreneurial insight and ideas we have to find ways to uncover and unlock these 'right' concepts.

More recently, Torill Bye Wilhelmsen set up her wonderfully named venture Fjellflyt, or 'Mountain Flow' in English, after a period of extreme burnout and associated illness. Working with business leaders and entrepreneurs in the Lom district of Norway, Wilhelmsen noticed that they were regularly expected to work 55 hours per week or more on their computers and that they felt not doing this was cheating in some way. Immersed in this environment, she quickly fell into some of the same traps. The Lean Startup methodology many of them followed and had somewhat driven this work ethic had become not so much a framework for their success but a cage, trapping them in their virtual worlds, hunched over their laptops, hour after hour. To them, the idea of going for a walk felt like cheating and not work at all.

Having lived through this experience, Wilhelmsen started to reflect on the irony that walking is actually central to Norwegian identity and yet only 20 per cent of Norwegians regularly practice it. They all love the concept of Dalsnuten, the 'Sunday Hike', but for most, this just remains a concept, not a reality. As an antidote to this, Wilhelmsen embarked on a series of self-experiments with an aim to walk herself better and to walk herself creative. She walked old routes, new routes, over mountains, into woods, got purposefully lost, walked alone and with others to see what worked best for her creative mind and what she terms 'flow'.

This concept of 'flow' and the pleasure Wilhelmsen found in being lost reminds me of a passage written by Robert Macfarlane, in which he celebrates getting lost as 'Drift': 'Drift is always becoming. Drift has unbounded potential. ... Drift happens to you rather than you to Drift.' These personal results of Wilhelmsen's experiments now form the core part of her ventures, offering, inviting and taking leaders and entrepreneurs on 'Walkshops' and encouraging them to integrate simple walking activities as a key element of their working schedules. She suggests they do this through taking two- to 20-minute walks throughout the day and having short, five- to six-minute walking meetings whenever they can. On her Walkshops, she finds a new democratic dynamic within teams develops, that the old, office-based rules break down to some degree and hierarchies relax, bringing an excess of 'Overskudd' (a lovely Norwegian word for 'profit', which also means excess energy) to the businesses she takes. No wonder once tried, her customers come back for more and more – Overskudd is a drug of sorts.

On the journeys I lead with executives, teams and groups I always aim to help participants find the optimal speed and tempo required to unlock their Outside Thinking by consciously taking away as many obstacles to this as I can. I only give minimal details of the route and length, quietly take responsibility for all navigation and pause, stop and get in sync with the effort involved on different terrains. In fact, the optimal tempo comes naturally to us as humans and is somewhat hardwired into our physiology. Put simply, don't rush, work moderately and adapt this to the terrain – no lung-busting rushes to bag a peak, but we take our time, pause and take in the views.

How long should we do this for?

Next for us to consider is time. How long should we give ourselves in order to get the real cognitive benefits of Outside Thinking? Should we walk, talk and think every day? Is a short walking commute enough, or do we need more immersive experiences? The studies we discussed earlier focused on testing Restoration Attention Theory, identified massive benefits that came after spending four days in nature, but do we need to give it this long? And, with pragmatism in mind, most of us will never find time to do this regularly within our working weeks.

Michael Easter* doesn't think we need to always give it too long and I'd agree. After what was to become a seminal trip for him to the Alaskan wilderness, his 'mind (felt) more like it belonged to a monk after a month at a meditation retreat. I just felt better.' Intrigued by this realization and inspired by what biologist E. O. Wilson put as, 'Nature holds the key to our aesthetic, intellectual, cognitive and even spiritual

*Easter, M. (2021). *The Comfort Crisis: Embrace Discomfort to Reclaim Your Wild, Happy, Healthy Self.* Rodale Books.

satisfaction', once back home, Easter called upon Rachel Hopman, PhD, a neuroscientist at Northeastern University, to try and understand what had happened. Hopman led a study[*] and along with other related researchers was instrumental in defining what they called the '20:5:3 Rule'. Think of this as being like your five-a-day fruit and vegetable rule, in that it attempts to define the minimum time everyone should spend in nature to get real cognitive benefits.

It works like this: Hopman and her colleagues propose that everyone should spend 20 minutes three times a week in natural setting, five hours per month somewhere semi-wild and three days a year totally immersed in nature. Just taking a 20-minute walk outside in nature, whether a wild wood, coastal path or just a tree-filled city park, is how long Hopman says it takes to enter the 'soft fascination' state, where we experience a restorative phase, process information, reduce stress levels and improve our executive skills. But, and here's a rub, this doesn't really work if you're interrupted by your phone or similar tech, so leave it at home or at the office. In Hopman's study, those who walked with their phone on saw none – yes, none – of these benefits.

*Hopman, R.J., Lotemplio, S.B., Scott, E.E., McKinney, T.L., Strayer, D.L. (2020). 'Resting-state posterior alpha power changes with prolonged exposure in a natural environment'. *Cognitive Research: Principles and Implications* volume 5, Article number: 51.

Maybe we should do what the Finns do? Which is generally pretty good advice for any area of life, I find. In 2005 a survey[*] of Finns revealed that those who spent a minimum of five hours each month in the wilderness were healthier and happier than those who didn't. A 2014 follow-up experiment[†] funded by the Finnish government took three groups and sent them off walking in three locations – a city centre, a city park and a forest. The results showed that the forest walkers got by far the most benefit out of this experience, both for their well-being and for their cognition. We've explored quite a few of the physiological, evolutionary and neurological reasons this might be, but Hopman also has a hunch that the actual physical nature of nature plays a part here. In nature you are surrounded by fractal patterns (the repeating patterns seen on leaves and plants) unlike in perpendicular buildings and cities, and it turns out our brains love fractals. We are subconsciously always looking for patterns and this in turn triggers interesting mechanisms in our brains. Why are so many people drawn to abstract art, such as that of Jackson Pollock? Fractals.

[*]Tyrväinen, L., Pauleit, S., Seeland, K., & de Vries, S. (2005). 'Benefits and uses of urban forests and trees.' In K. Nilsson, T. B. Randrup, & C. C. Konijnendijk (Eds), *Urban forests and trees in Europe*: A reference book (pp. 81e114). Springer Verlag.

[†]Tyrväinen, L., Ojala, A., Korpela, K., Lanki, T., Tsunetsugu, Y., Kagawa, T. (2014). 'The influence of urban green environments on stress relief measures: A field experiment.' *Journal of Environmental Psychology*.

In my own experience the second and third days of being in nature are immeasurably more transformative than the first. I simply put this down to the need to decelerate on day one and having already discussed Rosie Walford's retreats, Ruth Atchley's creative reasoning experiment and the experience of the military veterans, it should come as no surprise that there are really proven benefits to spending three or more days immersed in nature. If the previous two targets can be compared to your five-a-day targets, this stage can be thought of as being like your New Year detox (your Dry January). This bit is what really gets your brain into its default state, you get the full restorative benefits and your creative thinking starts to sparkle. Hopman suggests that this is a full retreat into the wilderness, far away from our phones, computers, bright lights and TVs and the other distractions of modern work and life. And, with explorer Belinda Kirk's thoughts in mind, even the planning and anticipation of this type of 'adventure' can have huge benefits before you even step foot on to the forest or mountain path.

The 20:5:3 rule is accessible, useful, practical, something we can all aspire to and perhaps start to work towards and integrate into our working lives and venture models. In the next chapter, I'll come on to my thoughts and methods on how to do this, but from my own experience and experimentation, I also believe that a structure like this can do so much more than restore us and can be managed and used as a powerful tool for innovation.

Make it a habit

One of the appealing aspects of Michael Easter and Rachel Hopman's work is that it combines both length and frequency into an easy-to-understand and, hopefully, achievable target to help us embed walking and the outdoors into our working lives. To begin to reap the benefits of this activity, I suggest you aim to build the following into your working life. Remember, this is work, not bunking off! Avoid weekends – these are for family, friends, eating, drinking, dancing, reading and fitness perhaps. If doing these things involves walking and nature, all the better but this is a bonus and not work.

Try this:

Twenty minutes daily, Monday to Friday

This is the easy bit and only needs loose planning: just turn off your phone, get away from your desk and walk a bit every single day. A city park is OK, taking the footpath instead of the street is good, woods and hills better. This can be alone as your commute to the office, or a *faux commute* to your home office, as a quick escape before or after regular meetings, or over a lunch break and is a powerful grounding and mind-clearing exercise, whether alone, with a colleague or as a team.

Three hours every fortnight

Every two weeks, schedule a morning or afternoon walk in a natural setting – over hills, through woods, along the coast, the canal, whatever is within easy reach. Plan a route, find a practitioner to lead you, join a local netwalking community, invite like-minded colleagues or clients, or take your team out yourself and get out for a three-hour walk. Someone in your team will probably relish the responsibility for organizing this. For solo or team walks, schedule this immediately before a regular meeting, like a board or strategy meeting – I guarantee you'll find quickly that they'll be much more effective and pleasurable as a result.

Three days every quarter

Rethink your offsite strategy days, cancel that conference in a soulless meeting room and forget about any residual guilt about this being a holiday. Organize and plan a three-day, two-night escape from the office with your team or colleagues every quarter. Or, if you work alone, join an organized trip. You may well need to find a facilitator or organizer and there are plenty around if needed to help you plan and organize logistics and routes in the great outdoors. This doesn't have to be a huge challenge but it can be if you're up for this. It doesn't need to involve wild camping or hardship, it can be point-to-point, or centre-based, but should be out in nature, somewhere away from technological distractions. As Ruth Atchley and her colleagues discovered through experimentation, this is the bit that has huge benefits to your cognitive function and creative thinking.

The working week should contain your walking week, not as an extra, nice to do, but as an integral part of your schedule.

Walking and talking works

Key to the effective use of walking for thinking are the changes and benefits that side-by-side conversation bring to communication as opposed to face to face. In 2020, Sara Cook and Christian van Nieuwerburgh ran a pilot project[*] to explore the benefits, often verbalized, that professional coaches experienced with clients in outdoor sessions. These included observations that clients tended to talk more freely, having greater insight, clarity and understanding. They found that for most, the experience was less intense than traditional meeting environments and there was a greater sense of equality. Reflecting on these reported personal experiences, I certainly find that the inherent and imagined hierarchies

*Cook, S., van Nieuwerburgh, C. (2020). 'The Experience of Coaching Whilst Walking: A Pilot Study.' *The Coaching Psychologist*, Vol. 16, No. 2.

of team structures tend to break down in teams I lead in the outdoors.

Cook and van Nieuwerburgh organized their findings into four key themes:

Theme 1: Openness to experience

The word repeated by most respondents was 'creativity' and participants provided feedback such as, 'Walking in the outdoors, there is an implicit spontaneity and freedom to that, which allows me to be more spontaneous.'

Theme 2: Awareness of body and mind

Participants reported increased awareness of their senses and felt more 'present', with one reflecting, 'It gives a sense of freedom, with no boundaries … there are no limits to what may become of my time spent in nature.'

Theme 3: Love of the outdoors

The simple experience of being outdoors was powerful for many participants, with one saying, 'Being out in the fresh air made me feel more able to organize my thoughts and vocalize my feelings.'

Theme 4: Being side by side

Strengthened by the first three themes, the enhanced sense of equality by physically walking side by side has noticeable effect on the positive outcomes of the participants' experiences.

There is lots of talk, and generally, we all naturally know about being outside and its benefits to our souls and our minds. Increasingly, walking and outdoor therapies are being prescribed by doctors for a wide range of illness and ailments. The growing body of research we have covered in this chapter is starting to combine to scientifically describe the tangible and measurable impact on creativity and problem-solving when participants spend time, and walk, in nature and this can and does have direct, measurable and tangible benefits to the organizations and ventures we work in.

When talking to prospective clients about the journeys and trips I organize for high-performing teams, there is often a focus on place, on where can or will we do this work. As you'll have garnered from reading my book so far, the answer to some degree is that it doesn't matter so long as it is in 'nature' in its broadest sense and I have given you some ideas of where to start doing this above. But in truth, it does matter – some places and environments are just better for getting the most out of Outside Thinking.

'As you sit on the hillside, or lie prone under the trees of the forest, or sprawl wet-legged by a mountain stream, the great door, that does not look like a door, opens.'
Stephen Graham, *The Gentle Art of Tramping*, 1923

The 'door' Stephen Graham talks of is of course a mental or cognitive one and I think he is referring to his imagination and not just a sense of well-being or relaxation. The bigger the place, the less boundaries of the space, the deeper and darker the forest or energetic the mountain stream, the more the door opens. These places get us into what Torill Bye Wilhelmsen earlier referred to as 'flow' and it is where we really reap the rewards. This doesn't mean we have to plan trips to the depths of the Yukon or the bleak peaks of the Scottish Highlands but can seek out the closer-to-home 'wild places' and there are a surprising amount of these left in the world.

Author Robert Macfarlane has sought out his *Wild Places**[*]* throughout the British Isles, exploring and experiencing deep, ancient woodlands, wind-blown peaks, snowy moors and clifftops. He has walked through them, slept in them, swam their waters and writes poetically about his experiences. Having done so, his understanding of wildness changed. As he says, 'I had learned to see another type of wildness, to which I had been blind: the wildness of natural life, the sheer force of ongoing organic existence, vigorous and chaotic. There was as much to be learned in an acre of woodland on a city's fringe as on the shattered summit of Ben Hope.'

Gerdi Verwoert is a coach who focuses on self-leadership and guides busy managers, executives and coaches who are stuck in the frustrating and stressful doing of everyday life and work into the quiet, expansive mountains of the Alps to

*Macfarlane, R., (2007). *The Wild Places*. Granta.

help them connect and reconnect with nature, themselves and what life to them is all about. Verwoert certainly thinks that mountains are a magical place; uniquely suited to help us slow down, be present and get a different perspective on life. As she puts it, 'What do you think when you unexpectedly come to a fork in a trail you're on? When you see one trail is obviously well-travelled while the other one is not? Do you continue without another thought along the well-travelled one? Or are you curious about the other one and at the very least tempted to explore it? When you've always travelled on trails that have been walked by many before you, it can be a daunting and even scary undertaking to leave it. To leave the beaten track, you have to trust you've learned enough to now safely navigate your own path. To leave the well-beaten trail means stepping into the unknown. It means others questioning your capabilities and the wisdom of your choice; projecting their insecurities and fears onto you. Only you can decide whether you're ready to carve out your own trail through life.'

Whether we have access to a city park, a river or canal, a local hill, mountain peaks, moorland, woodland, beaches, clifftops or coastal paths, we can all find our own wild places and open the door to our own creativity to discover our own and new paths to innovation and entrepreneurial success.

The outdoors can certainly make us healthy, it can also make us happy, sometimes ecstatically so, but it can also make us successful. My friend Ed Van Rooyen has made this

his, and his companies' mantra – HeHaSu – healthy, happy, successful. This is probably the best mission statement I've ever seen. It's what everything the company does hangs off, it's the goal of the founders and staff and it's their goal for their customers. Their work goes well beyond walking and the outdoors to include diet, fitness, mental health and much more, but through 'taking it outside', Ed and his team have found new ideas, clarity of thought, bonded and aligned as a team and generated real innovation and rapid growth of their venture.

And, as we've seen, many a true genius, whether writer, philosopher, mathematician or tech entrepreneur, has found their inspiration through walking. Along the way in researching and writing his fantastic book exploring how and where creative brilliance flourishes, *The Geography of Genius**, Eric Weiner meets a man, Swaminathan in Calcutta, who perhaps sums things up better than any genius has, 'Walk. Get up early, at dawn, and just start walking. Don't take a lot of money, don't have a destination in mind. Just walk. Don't stop walking. You might have an epiphany.'

We can all do this. Ignore all the science if you like, forget the anecdotes and quotes and just accept that real, deep, innovative work simply happens better outside. Then get yourself and your teams outside. Don't put it off. Just do it. Now.

*Weiner, E. (2016). *The Geography of Genius*. Simon and Schuster.

Five Walks That Changed My Thinking

5. Imlil, Morocco, 2018

Morocco is the spiritual home of Outside Thinking – it's where it came together for me. I'd been an entrepreneur, I'd been an archaeologist, I'd been a start-up advisor and I'd trained as a walking leader and it all came together for me in the autumn of 2018 in Morocco. The wife of one of my oldest and closest friends asked me to organize and lead a surprise hiking trip for a group of him and his friends for his 50th birthday. I'd visited and trekked in Morocco before, including for my honeymoon, so suggested it as a destination and luckily, his friends were all up for it. I took it upon myself to organize everything so they could all just turn up and see what was in store for them.

Apart from Richard, I didn't know the others well or at all. Through the course of three days trekking in and around Mount Toubkal, fording mountain streams, crossing high passes, trudging through rain, dipping our feet in freezing pools and picnicking in high meadows, I got to know them all better than I ever would have at a party. Our conversations were often silly, but often deep and thought-provoking too. A team was formed through shared experience. Many of them reflected that new ideas had formed, thoughts had become clear and they'd go home with a clearer sense of the future.

Outside Thinking was born.

CHAPTER SIX

Making Outside Thinking a Habit

'Whenever I need to do some serious thinking, I go for a walk in the woods.'

Calvin and Hobbes

I've included quite a few quotes within these pages and many serious philosophers and writers may have put it in slightly more verbose or loquacious language, but perhaps the young, wise Calvin sums up the core thesis of my book better than I ever will, but he's certainly not alone in knowing this.

As we've discovered through the course of this book, he is in good company – George Shackle, Saras Sarasvathy, Adam Grant, Jack Kerouac, Per Davidsson, Sara Elias, Gilles Deleuze, Félix Guattari, Will Herman, Anton Chekhov, Benjamin Baird, John le Carré, Julia Cameron, Jonny Ohlson, Joe Stringer, Austin Kleon, Mark Zuckerberg, David Eagleman, Paul Smith, Dimo Dimov, Marty Neumeier, Ken Robinson, Murli Nagasundaram, Bob Bostrom, Brian Mullen, Elspeth McFadzean, Michael di Paula, Patrick Lencioni, Jason Hayes, Joseph Allen, Richard

Mabey, Caroline Williams, Robert Macfarlane, Shane O'Mara, Rachel Kaplan, Steven Kaplan, Michael Easter, Brian Barnard, Derrick Herbst, Ruth Atchley, Jean-Jacques Rousseau, Frederic Gros, Belinda Kirk, Steve Jobs, Dave Stewart, Ed Van Rooyen, Fi Macmillan, Mia Keinänen, Rosie Walford, Torill Bye Wilhelmsen, Rachel Hopman, Sara Cook, Christian van Nieuwerburgh, Stephen Graham, Al Kennedy, Gerdi Verwoert and too many more I've met along the way to mention – researchers, academics, entrepreneurs, coaches, founders, investors, philosophers, writers, artists, explorers ... they're all striving to generate creativity, innovation and many of them, through accident or action, have discovered what Friedrich Nietzsche knew and articulated so well: Go outside. Freewheel. Be Distracted. Get lost. Talk side-by-side. Go for a walk. Think clearly.

Reflecting back on Nietzsche's quote that opened my book, 'Sit as little as possible. Give no credence to any thought that was not born outdoors while moving about freely,' we can see that it embodied two vital elements that we can all easily use to make Outside Thinking part of our everyday, working lives. Firstly, don't sit at your desk too much, don't believe that inspiration will somehow radiate from your screen, appear from surfing another website, sitting on another group Zoom call, tweaking another spreadsheet or through arriving early, or staying late, at the office. This ingrained mindset needs to be shifted to allow us all to bunk off, slow down, have different conversations and go outside. Secondly, we need ways to question and critique any idea that is born of or comes from our traditional working ways. Even if we do eventually bear them some credence, at least give them some air first. Ponder them. Interrogate them. Talk them through with friends and colleagues. But, most importantly, take them outside.

The novelist John le Carré knew this too, famously saying, 'a desk is a dangerous place from which to view the world', a quote I've pretty much commandeered for my own marketing purposes. Perhaps le Carré was himself inspired by Nietzsche, given the setting of his last, posthumously published novel, *The Villa Silverblick*, in Weimar, where the dying Nietzsche had spent his final years.

Over the years, through trial and error, I definitely found my thinking 'space' and continue to find inspiration outside, walking in the hills, mountains and coastal paths of the UK, Europe and North Africa – with the absolute appreciation that my desk is a dangerous place from which to view the world. And I call on anyone who aspires to be an entrepreneur, leader, fresh air thinker, idea explorer, tech innovator, creative or business activist to do the same.

It is time to do business differently

It is time to do business differently. Take your thinking outside and start Outside Thinking.

The time for research, analysis, stories, anecdotes and me chattering on about all of this is over and now we'll look at solid ideas, methods and techniques to make Outside Thinking a habit.

We've learned that almost no one does their best thinking in the office or sat at their desk. Almost everyone I've spoken to about this gets it. They know it already. And almost all already know that fresh air and the outdoors is the place where they get inspiration, do their best thinking and incubate new ideas. Often what they don't always accept or realize is that this is real, deep work – it's not bunking off.

Given our physiological, psychological makeup, our evolutionary history and the biochemical changes we go through when walking outside, this should come as no surprise to anyone who has looked into it, read the research or experienced it. Immersion in nature, even fleetingly, starts to put our minds into the all-important default mode; the state in which our brains start to fizz, make new connections and new ideas are born. This can give us an enormous sense of well-being and can also cure burnout, both mental and physical, in some people, but it's so much more than this.

The removal of the boundaries, physical, mental and metaphorical, that we experience outside, directly translate and influence our thinking. The outside is full of metaphor for our thoughts – spoken, unspoken, cheesy and transcendental. We have different conversations when outside, side-by-side, the narrative changes and stories materialize. We unlock our Outside Thinking. And, to make the accountants happy, it's a ridiculously cost-effective route to creativity, innovation, well-being and productivity.

To sum it all up in one mantra: *Go outside and meet people.*

Appendices

This is Powerful Stuff

On the trips I lead, and when meeting others working in my field, I always ask for feedback on the simple question of what the effects of being outdoors had on the participants' thinking. Here are some of the comments:

'It has been my refuge, my inspiration. A place of peace (often right in the middle of a storm).'

'I felt that we achieved more in casual conversation than hundreds of Zoom calls combined.'

'It made us all realize that sometimes we need to push ourselves and take on new challenges rather than staying in our comfort zones if we want to reap the reward.'

'It is hard to switch off from demanding notifications and tasks, but walking gives me peace. I don't find walking in the countryside has ever given me any great "aha" moments, but it stills my thoughts and allows my mind to incubate on the things I've been thinking about or working on, which then benefits me when I'm back at my desk. I just focus on my footsteps, on the whereabouts of the dog, on the light, sounds and smells around me. If anything, my mind is blank, which is a blessing in itself.'

'Blue sky is there to inspire you. With wisps of white cloud to wow you. The green landscape makes you wonder at nature, whilst you wander and do your best thinking.'

'I remember how balanced and collegiate conversations became when you're puffing along with someone, so you have to yield to the other person whilst you catch your breath and there are healthy silences, whilst you both think and negotiate a steep bit. Plus, of course you get conversations which last all day and are matched to a landscape. It suggests we are doing meetings all wrong, doesn't it?'

'Outside thinking for me is a way to get more creative. There is lots of space around you to help an idea grow. Add in that your mind has the opportunity to decompress as random but welcome moments like a bird call, the scent of damp soil, the sight of an unusual insect, the brushing past a dew-filled branch capture your attention and often your awe. You then step into the possibilities of what you may be able to create through interacting with nature.'

'For one, I find I can stop thinking. Outdoors, in a forest, along the ocean, sitting by a river, walking a path, nature invites me to be mindful of every little thing, concentrate, focus. I experience a great slowing down – breathing slows, walking slows, heart rate slows. I see differently, beginning with the old growth trees and then all the way down to mosses, mushrooms, critters.'

'I believe that one of the values of going out into nature is the listening. Because to listen to yourself and what you believe (and not what everyone else has taught you to believe), you need to listen to yourself like you listen in nature. Not listening to understand – not listening to relay something back to nature about your opinion. But just listening. To me, nature helps me find a way back to deep listening.'

'In those two days we had the best conversations as a team that we'd ever had, we spoke as real people, not just work colleagues.'

'It sounded a bit cheesy to be honest, but in reality, using the landscape around us as metaphors for the problems and opportunities we faced was incredibly powerful and has stuck in my mind ever since. I'm not sure we'd have got close doing some traditional blue sky thinking. Actual blue skies made all the difference.'

'The whole day was really powerful, punctuated with profound moments. People connected and reconnected with each other (and in one or two instances, with themselves) in a way that our experience suggests would have taken two to three times as long in an indoor space.'

Making It a Habit – The 20:3:3 Rule

The trick now is to make this a habit, not a 'nice to do' or an 'I do it when I can' type of thing. Not something to be re-scheduled because 'something important has come up' or because of the weather. It is important in its own right and needs to be built into our own habits, our teams' agendas and our venture's DNA.

Earlier, I introduced you to the 20:5:3 rule for walking – 20 minutes a day, five-hour long walk per month and three-day wilderness trip per year – and my suggested tweak to a 20:3:3 rule – 20 minutes a day, three-hour long walk every two weeks and three-day trip every quarter (*see also* pages 153–155). Following are some simple ways you can start to integrate the 20:3:3 rule into your working lives and organizational development.

Twenty-minute daily ideas

- Introduce a walking commute to work. Plan, if you can, four or five different 20- to 30-minute routes that you can choose from, dependent on weather conditions and time of year;
- Go a bit further for your coffee, smoothie or tea. Choose a coffee or lunch stop 10 to 15 minutes from your work and walk there and back;
- Take your one-on-one check-in meetings for a walk.

Three-hour fortnightly ideas

- Find and join a local netwalking group, start your own or suggest an existing networking group walk instead of meeting inside;
- Suggest a walking meeting to people you regularly meet, e.g. clients, advisors or coaches;
- Take your team meeting for a walk.

Three-day quarterly ideas

- Skip the conference centre and run your strategy retreat somewhere outside (check out some suggested itineraries later in the book, *see also* pages 218–234);
- Find and book a walking leader or facilitator like me to plan and guide you and your team on a trip;
- Research and book yourself on a group wilderness hiking trip and experiment with your own Outside Thinking.

Simply put, the more time you spend outdoors, exercising your Outside Thinking, the more ideas you'll have.

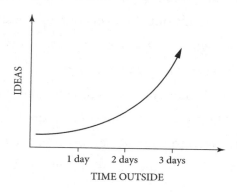

Whatever you strive for or achieve is a good start and platform to change your own and your colleagues' or team's thinking. However, remember that research by Brian Barnard and Derrick Herbst found that we need some processes or to use some semi-formal techniques in order to effectively generate new ideas or innovation while on these walks and outside. This is the core of Outside Thinking – the combination of the habit of walking and being outside with relevant creative thinking techniques to get your neurons firing effectively.

Rules of the game

Before we look at some specific, tried-and-tested techniques, let's consider more generally how to approach these walks, the spaces we'll travel through and the conversations we might have. My friend and fellow practitioner, Fi Macmillan, uses what she terms a 'SOFT' approach, which I like, I've adopted and use regularly. It goes like this:

S – Solo: Outside Thinking is for you and for your ideas, so whether you're actually out alone on your 20-minute daily walk or with six colleagues on a longer trip, keep this in mind. It's good to walk silently for a while, to slow a little, pretend to tie your shoelace and enjoy some solo time in your own thoughts.

O – Open: Always come outside with an open mind, open to your thoughts, open to your senses, open to the conversations you might have. Part of the beauty of doing this is not to be bound by an agenda or your to-do list so don't try to organize your thinking, just be open to what comes.

F – Freewheeling: Using Outside Thinking, we're aiming to be inspired by distraction. One of the easiest ways to achieve this is not to worry too much about your route before setting off, or better still, join a netwalking group or employ a walking leader who can deal with all of that for you. I'll cover some techniques you can use to help with this later.

T – Tech-free: This is important. Of course, keep your phone with you for emergencies and use it for taking photos or even navigating, but put it on airplane mode or silent and don't even think about looking at emails or taking calls while you're out.

Fi's SOFT approach is a useful mental reminder each time you go out and can quickly get you in the right frame of mind to begin to unlock your Outside Thinking.

Where to Practice Outside Thinking

In terms of where you walk and think outside, nowhere is the wrong place and everywhere can bring specific benefits or ideas of how to 'use' the space you're in.

Park life

A city park offers a unique juxtaposition between the outside and the inside. You may literally be able to see your office or home, the park may be alongside industrial areas, train tracks or a car park. Many of us have strong childhood memories associated with parks like these – the swings and sandpits, trees that were climbed and hidden places where dens were made. Parks are a place to view and experience nature alongside the bustle of human life and often to observe nature literally breaking through the built environment – saplings bursting through cracks in walls, grass claiming back asphalt. This can make parks excellent spaces to draw out your lateral, or sideways, thinking and a highly efficient place for a daily commute, short thinking walks, team get togethers or client meetings.

Take me to the river

Most of us have relatively quick access to a river, whether big or small, or even a canal, that we can follow on a walk. The

Avon River that runs through my hometown offers plenty of opportunities for walking, and in less than two miles from the centre of town you will find yourself in a relatively wild environment, where the river is overgrown and herons and kingfishers rule. On more back-country trips, I'll often divert a group I'm leading off-path to follow a stream from its source as it tumbles down the mountainside in a series of waterfalls, pools and rapids. The flow of a river mirrors Torill Bye Wilhelmsen's concept of 'Flow' that I discussed earlier (*see also* page 147), which, through adopting, allows our minds to drift rapidly into the default state we need to effectively think creatively.

Climbing up on Solsbury Hill

They say the best view comes after the hardest climb, but I don't entirely buy this. For me, it's all about perspective and vistas. A hill doesn't need to be particularly high, and it definitely doesn't have to require any climbing skills, it just needs to be high enough to rise above the surroundings in some way. Just being at the top of something changes your visual perspective, whether that is a full, expansive, 360-degree view to the horizon, a long view down a river valley, the unexpected site of the next, higher hilltop, or (as Peter Gabriel would have it), a lofty view of the city lights spread out below you. These are the landscapes where you can start to experience the benefits of having no boundaries.

Ain't no mountain high enough

Most people seem drawn to mountains for some reason, even if they never climb them themselves. It may be their simple majesty, their intimidating nature, the stories of conquering mountaineers or simply some deep desire to be at the top, perhaps summed up best by Robert Macfarlane in his book, *Mountains of the Mind* [ref], 'Mountains return to us priceless capacity for wonder which can so insensibly be leached away by modern existence, and they urge us to apply that wonder to our own everyday lives.'

Your mountain doesn't have to be Everest, the Eiger or even Ben Nevis. I've led almost countless people onto the summit of Pen y Fan in South Wales – for many their first proper peak – and at a modest 886 metres, some wouldn't even call it a mountain, but it has all of the metaphorical benefits of having no boundaries in bucketloads and is a perfect place for mentally broadening your horizons. So, my advice, get a guide and go up a mountain. And, if possible, ask them to take on a less-trodden path to the top – I love the feeling of leading a group up a minor route, where they probably won't have seen another soul all morning, over the lip on to a summit sometimes full of people who took the obvious path.

Between the saltmarsh and the sea

Coastal paths of any kind offer us liminal spaces, occupying a position at, or on both sides of, a boundary or threshold between solid land and the sometimes seemingly endless ocean. The seascapes and landscapes we can take in on these walks offer fresh perspectives and are full of rich metaphor. The sea has for many stirred the heart and inspired the imagination, as Austrian poet and novelist Rainer Maria Rilke put it, 'When anxious, uneasy, and bad thoughts come, I go to the sea, and the sea drowns them out with its great wide sounds, cleanses me with its noise, and imposes a rhythm upon everything in me that is bewildered and confused." Having to travel in one direction without much need for route finding helps our minds wander and our thoughts become clearer. Some of the most effective group trips I've led have been on coastal paths, often being battered by the wind and spray in the wildest weather.

Wide, open spaces

I grew up literally between two landscapes, where the tail end of a limestone escarpment petered out and met low, lying moorland stretching out to meet the sea, often in places lying lower than the sea itself, which was only held back by a long, low sea wall. The only building for miles was a single ancient cottage, seemingly inaccessible yet still perhaps occupied. This 'witches' house was the stuff of childhood nightmares. Maybe because of this I was always drawn inland to explore the hills,

*2018. *The Nature Lover's Quotation Book: An Inspired Collection for Hiking, Camping and the Great Outdoors.* Hatherleigh Press.

valleys and woodland. The moor seemed more intimidating and a somewhat other-worldly place. Nowadays I'm still drawn to the mountains but fully appreciate the bounded, but also boundarylessness of the moor, wide-open prairie or desert, where your eyes and mind are automatically drawn to the sky. It is almost meditative simply to walk through such a landscape.

Like a night in the forest

Like the mountains in springtime or a walk in the rain, a night, day or even a few hours in the forest or wood is a sure-fire way to fill up your senses, decelerate your mind and begin to think clearly and creatively. Even allowing for deforestation, 30 per cent of the land of Earth is still woodland or forest. Certainly, here in the UK and in most temperate areas, getting between some trees should be achievable for most.

My own garden backs on to a small area of wildwood, albeit only half a mile from the city centre. Here, I've placed a rusty, broken old bench, supported by a few rough-cut logs and rocks. It's my 'go to sit and think' spot. Just five minutes here, feeling the wind in the trees and hearing the birds, resets a busy mind between Zoom calls, writing or researching. The pathways through woodlands and forest tend to be numerous, from a wide logging track to a single-track route perhaps formed through the nightly commute of a badger or fox. These paths, offering no obvious destination or end, encourage us to literally try and see the wood from the trees as we contemplate our journey to date and our individual paths to the future. In summary, and as Cole Porter would have it, anything goes. Don't fret about where you practice Outside Thinking. At most, just have a think about where you can do so – anywhere outdoors offers a different perspective for your thinking and creativity.

When Can You Use Outside Thinking?

Embrace seasonality

You can read up on and investigate regenerative business models, biomimicry and related fields in other books and decide if they're relevant or useful for your business. I'd encourage you to do so as the natural world has much to offer business, way over and above my proposals for using it to generate creativity and new ideas through Outside Thinking. However, a very elegant element that can be really useful and powerful is simply to channel or reflect your conversations to mirror the seasons. These can apply to any of the methods and techniques outlined in my book through using them through a seasonal lens.

Winter: Hunkered down and wrapped up warm, the winter is a time for reflection and planning, to get everything right and ready for seed, grow and harvest through the rest of the year. Use the winter months to research, reflect on the previous year. Discuss questions and run activities with lenses such as:

(a)   What resources do we have available for the next year?
(b)   Are all of our functions running smoothly and efficiently?

(c) What research can we do to prepare ourselves for the coming year?

Spring: This is the season for preparing the ground and planting seeds, for an openness to what might be possible, for investigating all new ideas and beginning to sow the seeds for their later success. Not all will grow and succeed, but none will if never planted.

(a) Build, review and finalize product launch and development plans;

(b) Run kick-off meetings, team development session and do recruitment;

(c) Try out new things, be agile, test, break things and learn.

Summer: By summer, you'll know what is growing strongly, the fruits that are appearing, what you can prepare to harvest and will yield the greatest results. It may be a time to write off a crop (idea) and leave the field fallow until next spring, but it is also a time to recharge yourselves, sit in the sun and have a break before the hard work of harvest.

(a) What's not growing/developing and what is?

(b) How can we nurture and cultivate our successful products and services?

(c) Take team trips, decelerate, recharge ready for harvest.

Fall or Autumn: This is harvest season, so all hands to the deck to reap the rewards or perhaps to work on optimization, to refine your innovation and new ideas.

(a) Run fast, market hard, raise investment and close deals;

(b) Focus on efficiency and productivity;

(c) Reflect on the year's innovation and prepare for the next cycle.

The simple truth is that the outdoors is everywhere around us and getting out in it, walking, talking and thinking in it, is the easy bit. So just do it, whatever the environment you are or can be in.

What's the return on investment (ROI)?

As you've hopefully gathered through the book, there is plenty of supporting science in all this as well as our simple human experience, so the next stage is about introducing you to some structure, methods and techniques to unlock your Outside Thinking. Here are some I've experimented with, tried, tweaked, tested out on individual and teams and have got results. As tech CEO and serial entrepreneur Ed Van Rooyen reflected, 'We often talk about "return on investment" when it comes to business. Putting a price on having a more motivated and aligned self-aware team who have learnt some new life skills and since our walk come up with some amazing ideas resultant from the discussions and process that will stand the test of time is truly priceless. Pure genius and genuinely transformational.'

There certainly is profit or return on investment in generating new creative ideas and in the use of the outdoors and Outside Thinking to do this, whether that is simply through increased well-being from the alleviation of cognitive loads, directly through increased productivity through heightened focus or deeply through the generation of new innovative ideas.

Methods and Techniques

Having explored some of the ways to build and embed the outdoors into your working lives and your organizational development we now need to consider some methods and techniques to use those times to unlock some deep outside thinking. I've spent the last four years trailing and testing my practices with all sorts of teams in many locations and environments and have developed an assorted set of techniques I can dip into or build programmes around.

Over the following pages I'll introduce and explain some of these and offer some structured agendas for you to experiment with yourselves and with your teams. There is no right or wrong and these aren't supposed to offer any A to B type progression. Some are suitable for you to do solo, some more aimed at teams and some are better with some sort of facilitation. All I hope is that you try some, experience the unlocking of your own Outside Thinking and start to build some effective outdoors habits. Good luck!

Carry a question

Whether you've experienced some coaching, are a coach yourself or have just read up about the power of it, one of the keys is to carry a question with you. Outdoors, away from daily distractions and 'mechanical time', is the perfect place to carry a question and an ideal place to talk through these questions with your walking buddy, colleague or teams.

This isn't really a method or technique at all, but simply a call to think before you leave about a question, to write it in a notebook and let it lodge in your mind. Some of my favourite questions for Outside Thinking lend themselves to both individual reflection and creative thinking as well as in group or team environments and include:

1) Why do you/I do what you/I do?
2) What's the most important thing to me/you about what I/you/we do?
3) What do you/I want our business to be renowned for?
4) What is my/our business like when it's at its very best?
5) What are me/you and our team shit hot at?
6) What would I/we/you like to look back on in 100 days' time?
7) How afraid of our business are our competitors?

8) Do we/you really allow ourselves and our team(s) enough time to think and innovate?

9) Would I/you rather meet my/your 18- or 80-year-old self?

10) Are we in our investors shit bucket?

These should be pretty self-explanatory and I've found that most draw out a lot of related and tangential information once discussed. The last one perhaps requires some clarification! An investor friend of mine once said something that has stuck with me ever since and has offered me some insight into many investors' minds. He relayed to me that internally all of their investments were either stellar successes or in the shit bucket, there was no in between, no 'doing OK', no 'on the cusp'. It didn't mean that they'd totally written off those in the shit bucket, but that those that weren't got their disproportionate attention, support, help, introductions, PR and 'love'. And, it wasn't simply based on financial success or traction of a venture but mostly on their pace, energy and the excitement being generated around it.

What3Words

As we discussed earlier (*see also* pages 129–30), RAT (Remote Associates Test) is a tried-and-tested measure of creative reasoning – taking three seemingly un-associated words and attempting to come up with a meaningful fourth associated one. And, as we discovered, our ability to do this rises dramatically after a good walk (50 per cent in the case of Ruth Atchley's work and as much as 100 per cent in Marily Oppezzo's experiments).

What3Words is a fantastic geolocation tool that chops the whole world into a neat 3 x 3 metre grid. Every one of these cells is then allocated and identified by a unique three-word combination. For example, the Statue of Liberty can be found at planet.inches.most.

A great creative technique in the outdoors after a good walk is to combine these two things. It doesn't matter how many of you there are or where you are – up a mountain, in a wood, just outside your office – as you just need to be able to stand three metres apart, open the What3Words app and get each of your unique three words. Once you have these words, you have a few options:

Option 1: Use these words in a traditional RAT test by simply trying to come up with as many other words that could tie them together. As What3Words is so random this can be tough, so you could allow participants to move around, finding as many they can 'solve' in five or ten minutes.

Option 2: Ask participants to write a poem, haiku (a Japanese short form poem structure made up of three lines of five, seven and five syllables), or creative sentence or paragraph using these words in ten minutes. They can write more than one if they like and as an open creative task it can be on any topic or you could suggest one – e.g. the future, the planet.

Option 3: A tweak to the Option 2 but focused on your company or venture. This can be especially powerful around mission statements, marketing straplines by setting questions such as 'Why do you do what you do?', 'What does your company do?' and often brings out deep differences in the viewpoints of colleagues. For example, on a walkshop I led with a team from a deep tech, AI venture, two of the executives got these three words sat atop an Iron Age hillfort on a blowy autumnal day, and produced the following:

The CTO – girder.cure.shimmered

knowledge girder holds
shimmered worlds of datastuff
showing problems cure

The CEO – scarf.blotting.festivity

With COVID blotting out our normal seasonal festivities, wrap up with your scarf and gloves, and join us in the fresh air with fire pits

With their minds free through walking, perhaps this activity began to forefront issues they had already been germinating or had been nagging away at them in their respective roles. The CTO seems far more product focused and throughout the walk had been trying to find ways to communicate their complex solutions and span the What3Words to reflect this – 'girder' offering a metaphor for the robustness of their approach, 'shimmering' the cutting-edge allure and power of AI and 'cure' the key value proposition. Maybe a cure to an ill that clients don't even know they're suffering from. The CEO, on the other hand, was focused on the staff and team moral and the hope of coming out of a very challenging period.

Forest Dipping

I love sending teams I walk with into the woods, to sit, be silent, decelerate rapidly and quickly get their minds into, or towards, default mode.

Shinrin-Yoku or 'Forest Bathing' in English, is a Japanese therapy developed in the 1960s, although really something people had naturally practiced for ever. Studies on the health benefits of spending time among trees and in forest and woodland has demonstrated that this practice actually changes the nervous system through calming neuro-psychological effects. The stress hormone, cortisol, is reduced and our immune systems are boosted, blood pressure drops, concentration and mental clarity increase through this very simple act. The practice of Shinrin-Yoku as a therapy is spreading fast across the world but in reality, you can reap the key benefits easily and quickly yourself. Even 5 minutes seems to have a lasting effect on most people, 10 minutes is great and if you allow 15, then you might have to go and wake up some of your team lying on the forest floor.

I call it Forest Dipping as I use it as a short exercise early on in the walks I lead. Try this:

Step 1 – Plan a spot in woodland or forest 20–45 minutes into your walk. It is definitely more powerful after you've walked a bit already.

Step 2 – Phones off.

Step 3 – Wander into the woods, off the path and find whatever spot takes your fancy – leaning against a tree, lying on the forest floor, sitting on a log.

Step 4 – Be silent and simply take in your surroundings. Look more closely at a leaf, listen to the sounds around you, look up to the sky above the tree tops, notice your breathing.

Step 5 – If you're the leader, do the same, but set a timer. When the time is up, clap loudly or whistle to bring everyone back together and walk on. No need to discuss the experience.

The wildest ideas

Walt Disney very successfully employed a three-step process of Dreaming, Realism and Criticism to come up with some great ideas and products. The Dreamer's job was to be divergent and just come up with ideas, the Realist to sift through these and decide how they could be implemented and the Critic poses problems. And the cycle can keep going round and round to try and generate great new, but realistic and doable ideas.

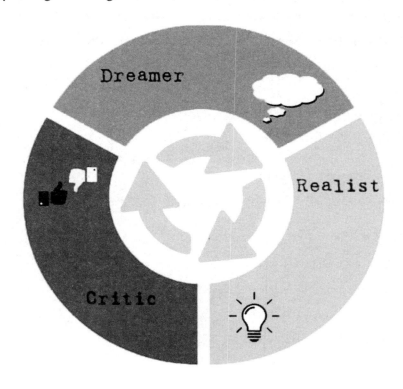

It is the Dreamer's wild imagination that opens the door to creativity and we know that the outside is a sure-fire shortcut to this. It's no wonder that being somewhere 'wild' generates 'wild' ideas but how do we actually stimulate our inner Dreamer and get our imagination firing and what techniques can help? Imagination more often than not is not restricted by ourselves but the environments we put ourselves in.

Try this technique yourself or with colleagues as it works brilliantly when integrated with or entirely done in the outside. The concept behind the technique is known as 'The Wildest Idea'. It sparks your lateral thinking by taking you to a position where you can look at the problem from a brand-new perspective. The benefits can be summed up as 'it's easier to tame down a wild idea than it is to invigorate a weak one'. This is a very good technique for unstructured problems – single questions or challenges – which require high doses of creativity. Examples might include:

- How can we replace our competitor's product?
- How can we get 1,000 new users in the next three months?

Step 1: Set a question that you or your team need to consider

This is the sensible step, i.e. discuss and agree or propose a valid, current and relevant question or challenge that your company, venture or team are facing.

Step 2: 15 minutes to be wild

Individually, come up with your wildest, most unrealistic solutions to the challenge. And the solutions should be particularly unrealistic, even impossible, illegal, unethical. Otherwise these solutions are not acceptable inputs for the next stage.

Step 3: Share your wild ideas

Get together and propose your ideas to each other. Propose your wild ideas and discuss them in detail as you would any 'sensible' idea – the pros, cons, the resources needed. Don't settle on anything here – anything still goes.

Step 4: Go for a walk

After (hopefully) a few laughs together, walk for 30–45 minutes. Undemanding tasks like walking generate mind-wandering, which in turn facilitates creative incubation, i.e. you get inspired by distraction. You don't need to explicitly think about the wild ideas, work or anything particular, just enjoy a dose of vitamin D and some fresh air.

Step 5: Bring it back down

Get back together and discuss the ideas again but with a heavy dose of realism. By looking at the problem from the point of view of the wildest idea, it can be easier to define realistic ideas which finally solve the challenge. These realistic ideas are the ones to be seriously considered for the final solutions to the challenges. You may reach a consensus on an idea to take forward or you may just shorten the list.

Step 6: Send in the critics

Now do the hard work and turn the potential solution(s) into workable plans, products or services.

Natural storytelling

So much of an entrepreneur's time is spent telling stories – to investors, to new hires, to customers, to partners, to wives, husbands, parents, partners, friends and random people they meet in trains or planes. The elevator pitch is a story, the pitch deck is a story, the new product pitch is a story, the meeting with the bank manager is a story, the sales presentation is a story ... Innovation has a narrative and is a story. Entrepreneurs can write these, tell them or get help doing this, but there is always benefit in exploring new ways to tell these stories. Staring for more hours at PowerPoint slides is rarely creative and as we've seen throughout this book, it is no surprise that walking in nature has been an inspiration to so many writers.

A quick-fire way through Outside Thinking to explore ways of telling your stories is through the use of found items:

Step 1 – For a portion of your walk, ask participants to look for, find and pick up any item they find interesting – a stick, a leaf, some moss, a plant, flower or lost item. Don't overthink it, just gaze while you walk and pick up whatever takes your fancy.

Step 2 – At a good stopping point, ideally somewhere open with some space to gather, get into teams of five or six.

Step 3 – Task each team to discuss, prepare and deliver a story using the objects. Give them 10 minutes to prepare before presenting to the rest of the team. The story can be about anything, but works really well if it is about their team (tell us about a recent achievement), a strategy, a customer journey or recent problem or setback. Note: this is a great exercise to capture on video and save to go back to at a later time.

Three Stones Make a Wall

Given my background, I had to get some archaeology in here! There is a saying in archaeology that 'Three stones make a wall', related to the interpretation of underground structures when excavating an archaeological site. Two stones in a line could represent a start of a wall or structure, but could mean nothing, whereas once you have three stones purposefully placed in a line then you probably have found something significant and worth excavation.

In many walks of life, the number three, sometimes called 'The Power of Three', is important and significant. In business spheres, it is often a cornerstone of marketing and creating effective copy and many of the most memorable mission statements include three key words. Metaphorically, this relates well to the archaeological addition of a 'wall'. Three well-chosen, strong words can build a metaphorical wall for your venture. A wall that helps you stand out from the competition, for example. The impact of the number three on human experience is undeniable. Three of anything seems to appeal to our brains and is often part of how we relate to the world, or at least used to communicate these relations. We often think in sets of three, such as:

- Past, Present, Future;
- Beginning, Middle, End;

- Here, There, Everywhere;
- You, Me, Them;
- Mind, Body, Spirit;
- Friends, Romans, Countrymen.

We can take and use The Power of Three in the outdoors and through using three stones, can integrate into our Outside Thinking.

At the start of, or early on in, a walk, I'll issue each participant with three small stones (anything from 3–6cm long is good), ideally gathered from, in or around the place we're in, so they have some relation and significance to this place. We'll then discuss a question they're pondering or an area of their business they want to discuss. Each participant is then asked to write a single word on each stone that means something in this context. They then pop them in their pocket and we walk. There is no need to chat about what they've written. At two significant points on the walk – a path junction, a hilltop, a point with an amazing view, a river crossing – I'll ask each person to discard one of their stones: the one they consider the least important or weakest. Some choose to hurl them into the air, some to place them carefully – it's a personal choice (I'm definitely a hurler). Towards the end of the walk, we pick another spot to rest and the team then pool their stones and see what words are left. Some may match, some may not, some may not make sense to the others. The team then discuss their choices, propose their rocks to be 'saved' and have to agree on the final three stones to keep.

If you need some question prompts, try these:

1) Using Past, Present, Future as a start, ask each participant to choose a word for each of these categories, perhaps related to the company or venture might be 'What were we good at?' (the Past), 'What are we best at now?' (Present), 'What should we be good at?' (Future).

2) Starting with You, Me and Them, pick one word to sum up what your customers would say about your product or venture (You), a word that reflects what you personally bring to this view (Me) and, finally, a word to sum up your customers' most important need (Them).

The Innovation Game

This exercise is inspired by the fantastic 2010 game, *Innovation*, created by Carl Chudyk. Central to this game are the assumptions that technological developments have been the defining factors in every historical period and that this is always accelerating. The world around us, and that we can walk through, is of course full of history, embodied in the landscape, in plain sight in buildings and industrial heritage and still defining many aspects of the commercial world (e.g. farming). This exercise involved either some planning or some knowledge of the environment you might be walking through (i.e. is there a hillfort, a railway, an old factory, a Greek temple even?). Do a little research into these features and have a few facts at your fingertips.

The actual exercise is simple enough – stop at an historical feature and pick one of the key technological developments listed below that matches the historical period. As a group, discuss how this development unfolded and affected history and if you were working on or launching your venture, business, product or idea at this time in history, what would it have looked like?

- The Prehistoric Period – Domestication of animals and plants, metalworking;
- The Classical Age – Mathematics, waterproof cement and canal building;
- The Medieval Age – Medicines, the compass, spectacles;
- The Renaissance – The printing press, telescope;
- The Exploration Age – Coal mining, banking, the sextant;
- The Enlightenment (1735–1819) – Atomic theory, canning and emancipation;
- The Romance Age (1820–94) – The railroad, refrigeration and the Theory of Evolution;
- The Modern Age (1895–1945) – Flight, Quantum Theory and skyscrapers;
- The Postmodern Age (1946–72) – suburbia, computers and satellites.

This is at core a group creative thinking exercise so don't try to be super specific or it can become quite hard to do. And, it's sometimes easier to start closer to the current time e.g. if you're a tech firm, what would it have been like to launch in the early nineties, just as the internet was getting going. Or focus on the core purpose of your product and then consider the technology available in a given time period and whether you could have delivered a version of your unique selling point (USP) within these limitations.

Go Get Lost

As a walking leader, I am certainly not advocating actually attempting to get purposefully lost, but I do see the advantages in purposefully not knowing where you're going. The mind-wandering and freewheeling effects of not caring about your route, destination or length of walk can be startling and take some practice. Many of us have experienced part of this on longer walks when sections and periods of time seem to disappear and we're just in the rhythm of walking and thinking. I often find this happens naturally when walking on coastal paths simply as route finding becomes irrelevant – simply follow the path with the sea on your left or right. Easy. But I'm rarely physically lost, just lost in thought.

As a leader, I try to help participants and clients get into this state by only offering them a meeting point by way of pre-trip information and nothing else. Having parked up and put their boots on, they'll often instantly ask me about the day's proposed route, length, height gain, difficulty, etc., but I resist and love the joy on their faces at the end of the walk as they stroll back into the car park or our destination (often a pub), not really knowing how they got there.

If on your own, or organizing a walk for your own team, especially straight from the office and not in some wilderness setting, try randomly picking a direction to walk in (spinning a pen on the floor is a simple way to do this), find what pathways you can, routes sticking as closely as you can to your direction of travel until you decide to stop. You can retrace your tracks, call an Uber or jump on a bus to get back.

A Pilgrimage, solo or as a collective

Earlier, we discussed some of the work of neuroscientist Shane O'Mara into the history, concept and benefits of pilgrim walking and how he believes that this can embody a metaphorical journey to a goal as well as a real journey to a destination and how it can be a powerful journey for a team or group to make together (*see also* page 124). But how can we build a sense of this into our normal working lives?

Through and during our work, most of us will have to attend client meetings, sales pitches, conferences, talks or board meetings. A little later, I'll cover some potential itineraries or agendas to take some of these events outside and embrace some Outside Thinking, but in terms of including an element of pilgrimage into your walking meetings, here are a few ideas:

1) **The preparation walk:** Before that important pitch, talk or presentation don't sit in the corner of a café cramming, knocking back another espresso or organize some pre-meeting, meeting. If you don't know your stuff now, it's too late. Much better is to 'commute' alone or as a group to that meeting on foot, walk from the train station straight into the room or set out on a circular walk from and back to your office immediately before it: actually walk into the meeting.

2) **Going back to our roots:** Did your venture start out in your bedroom, your living room, the corner of a co-working space, at the desk of a previous job or even at the beach on holiday? If so, take your colleagues, team, new hires or even customers on a walking pilgrimage there. It might take an hour or even a day, it doesn't matter. Use this walk to tell the story (maybe again) of your venture's origin.

3) **Places of inspiration:** Who, where or what has inspired you on your entrepreneurial journey so far? If I had to pick one person, it would be Yves Chouinard, founder of Patagonia. And it all started for him in his Tin Shed, his blacksmith's shop in Ventura, California. For a deep-tech venture perhaps, it might be CERN in Switzerland (at the cutting edge of particle physics), Stonehenge in the UK (embodies group co-operative effort), Venice (home of the Medici for global trade), Everest base camp (for determination), the Media Lab at MIT (innovation) or the Intel Museum in Santa Clara (to see the history of modern technology and visualize its constant acceleration and progress). So, take a team trip, organize a walking tour and soak up some inspiration.

4) **Viewpoints:** Maybe closer to home you can find inspiration simply through walking to and taking in a view.

The Nine-Point Problem

A play on the classic Nine-Dot Problem for use outdoors is a great opener for a trip outdoors to spark some creative thinking and teamwork, assuming at least some of your group don't know the possible solutions.

The Nine-Dot Problem is simple enough and designed to literally help us think outside of the box. Usually it is a paper exercise, with participants issued a pattern on nine dots in a grid:

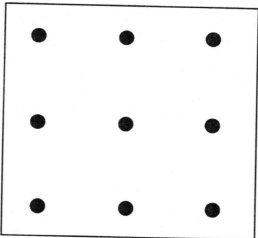

They are then asked to join all of the dots without lifting their pen or pencil from the paper, using three or fewer straight lines.

In the outdoors, this can be replicated in two ways:

1) Create a grid of nine rocks or sticks with approximately 2–3 metres between each one and task the team to walk the lines instead of drawing them.

2) If you have at least ten people in your group, replace the stones or sticks with them standing in position and have one person walk the lines and tag them as they pass.

I've deliberately not included any solutions. And you don't have to offer the solution if they can't solve it first time, walk on and try it again later once their creative reasoning skills are heightened.

No Boundaries

As we explored during the course of this book many of the boundaries that we habitually encounter in normal workplaces and the systemic activities we've been trained to think of as generating innovation actually limit creativity and team relationship building. In the outdoors, these are rapidly removed. The outdoors can create an immense sense of freedom, help to trigger significant shifts in perspective and simply enrich the nature of our conversations with one another. One of the key reasons for this is the real and metaphorical removal of boundaries: removal of the physical constraints placed on us by meeting and conference rooms, of sitting, of facing one another and metaphorically due to the seemingly limitless nature of the natural world.

A simple place to experience and explore this is on top of a hill or the summit of a mountain. On one trip I led, I asked the participants to simply find a spot at the top of the mountain summit we'd walked to, face North, stand still and focus silently on the horizon for two minutes, then turn and do the same to the South, East and West. It seems incredibly simple and yet is a powerful thinking tool. On one trip, a participant taking part in this exercise decided to do it while performing a headstand. As he put it, that way he was literally supporting the whole globe under his head like a metaphorical Atlas, but he also now had an entirely different perspective to everyone else.

Release your natural child

Central to Outside Thinking is the ability to get our minds into the all-important Default Mode and as we explored, as young kids we are often naturally in this state, but too often through our working environments have lost easy access to it. The outdoors can reset this and a simple way to accelerate this is to be more child-like. Forest Dipping (*see also* page 194) can do this, but you can also achieve it through some other simple activities:

- Lie on the ground and look at the sky and clouds for 10 minutes;
- Take off your walking boots and socks and paddle in a stream;
- Run, carefree, down a grassy slope;
- Scramble up a rocky hillside;
- Walk barefoot for a mile – dry grass, a sandy beach or soggy muddy trails are all good;
- Skim stones on a lake or at the sea;
- Flatten out a 'bed' in the long grass.

Don't be fooled by what might seem the infantile nature of these suggestions or their seeming simplicity, they really do work to rapidly change your cognition, outlook and thinking.

Walk in my shoes

Throughout this book, I've often referred to and outlined how many great philosophers, thinkers, writers and business visionaries have used walking for thinking to create amazing works of art, literature and radical innovation. And there are plenty more examples that I haven't mentioned yet. Here are just a few:

Søren Kierkegaard, nineteenth-century Danish philosopher, said, 'Above all, do not lose your desire to walk: Every day I walk myself into a state of well-being and walk away from every illness; I have walked myself into my best thoughts, and I know of no thought so burdensome that one cannot walk away from it.'

Seneca, one of the most famous Stoics and philosophers and also one of the richest men in the Roman Empire, suggested that, 'We must go for walks out of doors, so that the mind can be strengthened and invigorated by a clear sky and plenty of fresh air.'

Charles Dickens, Ludwig van Beethoven, Mark Zuckerberg, Jack Dorsey and many more all have used – or use – walking for thinking.

Dependent on where you are, do some research on some of those listed above and you'll be surprised at how many of their routes (or close enough to their routes) you can uncover. For example, Mark Zuckerberg walks to a scenic lookout above Palo Alto, Jack Dorsey's *wisdom walks* to the Gandhi statue in San Francisco and Charles Darwin's daily woodland strolls near his home in Kent, UK.

For the more adventurous of us with longer to commit, try walking, book in hand, in the footsteps of Cheryl Strayed on the Pacific Crest Trail, Bill Bryson on the Appalachian Trail, Raynor Winn's *Salt Path* on the south-west coastal path of the UK or any of Alfred Wainwright's beloved Lake District Fells.

Suggested Meeting Structures and Itineraries

Outdoor office day

Maybe you're not entirely sold yet and need an easy way to taste the benefits of Outside Thinking alongside others and to encourage your colleagues and staff that it's powerful stuff? A group of forward-thinking folk from the Netherlands have been on a mission for a number of years to do just that, through their Outdoor Office Day movement (https://www.outdoorofficeday .nl). It is simple: nothing to sign up for, just join teams and ventures across the world on a day in May or June each year and move your work outside. Even if you work on your own, or are self-employed, you could get your own group together of like-minded people and join the movement. Their tips to do this include:

1) **Take a walking meeting:** Simply schedule and move your meetings for this day outside, in a park or on a walk.

2) **Walk a new route to work:** Encourage everyone in your organization where possible to commute to work on foot, whether from home, from the car park, train or bus station, by taking a new route. Try to make this a 20–40-minute

route. Get together when you've all arrived at the office and share your routes and thoughts.

3) **Move tables, chairs and desks outside for the day:** This could be just outside your office if you have the space, into gardens and terraces for home workers, by booking an outdoor venue or even through flinging all the doors and windows to your workspace open and sitting right by them.

4) **Create a temporary terrace or your car park for meeting:** A more organized version of the previous tip if you have the space is to move whole teams into a temporary outdoor space to work for the day.

5) **Take your lunch for a walk:** The French have gone the whole hog and, in 2021, passed legislation* banning the eating of lunch at desks, but we can all at least do this for a day by picking up or packing a lunch and taking it on a walk, solo, in small groups or as a whole company.

6) **Get your coffee break drink at a café 10 minutes' walk away:** Break the coffee machine and office kitchen habit and don't go to the closest place for your latté or tea, but walk somewhere new, grab your drink and walk back to the office.

7) **Walk and talk on the phone:** Got an important call to make, then skip a video conference, leave our desk and talk while

*Article R.4428-19 of the 3,324-page French labour code, or *Code du Travail*

you walk. Although, please do look where you're walking though!

Do as much or little as you can of this, but best would be to embrace the concept fully and make it a whole organization thing. Combining this day with some of the other techniques I cover, or as a framework for a big meeting, will make it even more powerful.

Outside Strategy Day

We all need days such as this and I hope I've convinced you to do something different and not revert to booking another soulless meeting room or conference centre. You could go properly wild and run this somewhere in the deep countryside, but even the right hotel or outdoor centre could offer a mix of indoor and outdoor space and scope for a walkshop. By combining a walkshop into your off-site strategy days your whole team can share a real and deep metaphorical journey centred on your venture or organization. Don't overplan these days and accept that in a one-day planning session or meeting you have time for just three or four important conversations. These might include:

- Vision: Where are we going?
- Mission/purpose: Why do we exist? Who is the customer we serve?

- Strategic priorities: What do we need to focus on to achieve our vision?
- Specific questions around sustainability, ethics or innovation strategies.

Here is a draft agenda and plan for an Outside Thinking strategy day. If you have the right team members, you can likely put this together yourselves, or if not, find and hire a facilitator to run it for you. The right venue can certainly help with the practicalities.

Draft agenda

- **'Fireside' Chat:** Informal start to the day, meet and greet, maybe around the firepit, but can be on the terrace of a venue. A chance for the leader or facilitator to set out the agenda.
- **Key presentations 1:** This can be flexible, indoors with all of the traditional meeting-room tech or, if you're braver, verbal-only presentations outdoors. Each key team make a short presentation (15 minutes each) on how did we get here?, what have we done well?, how can we improve?
- **Outdoor Whiteboard:** Leave the tech behind if you used it, set up a whiteboard outside and review results, mission or vision. Just collect key words.
- **Key Presentations 2:** Back to the presentations. Each team should address the question, where are we going?
- **Outdoor Lunch:** Leave it at that and have lunch outside. A packed lunch, delivered by a local trader, or a light meal made on the fire perhaps.

- **Walkshop:** Now it's time to walk. Plan and set out on approximately a 90- to 180-minute country walk, including stops, with notebooks and pencils, and stops. Dependent on the countryside you are in, you could cover in open discussion:
  - **In the woods:** Wood vs trees, reminding ourselves as to the benefits and how we will keep them in view.
  - **At a river or waterfall:** The joys of running agile, are we agile enough?
  - **At a stile, steep climb or river crossing:** Looming obstacles (people, process, tech, data, competition), what is standing in our way?
  - **At the top of a hill or somewhere with a good view:** No boundaries, what could we do without any boundaries or obstacles in the way?
  - **In a farm field or meadow:** How do we farm our opportunities? Are we planting and nurturing enough new 'crops'?
  - **At the castle, ruin or old building:** What walls have we put up between teams? How can we break these down?
  - **In the clearing:** 'Blue sky thinking'. If resources were unlimited, what would we want to do?
  - **Paths in the woods:** Individually, what do we bring and what could we improve to clear a path?
  - **Take a break:** Remember to take a break every 30 minutes!

- **Indoor whiteboard wrap-up:** A session back in the meeting space to capture reflections from the walkshop and define next steps and actions.
- **Optional evening:** Time to relax, socialize and eat outdoors.

Remember, many of the activities outlined previously can be built into the walkshop stops and natural environments you find yourself in.

On a Mission of 3

Outside Thinking is a powerful technique for revisiting, exploring, tweaking or rewriting your ventures mission or value statement. Try this half-day itinerary to do just that:

Planning: Plan a circular walking route that allows, dependent on the ability of your team, for minimum three hours of walking and allow a total of five hours excluding travel to and from the start point. Aim to choose a route that has at least different environments and at least one hilltop, summit or viewpoint. Ensure at least one of you has the What3Words app (*see* page 225) installed on your phone.

Meet: Meet at the starting point, check kit and issue each participant with a blank pocket notebook (A5 or smaller) and a waterproof pen or pencil. If you have a mission statement already that you plan to review or improve, ask everyone in the group to write this down in their notebook. Don't have one yet?

Give each member three minutes to write a possible statement. It doesn't matter how good this is, polished or even complete. Don't share these, just pack up and start walking.

Ten to 15 minutes in: Stop once away from the starting point somewhere you can spread out and find an individual spot (a woodland setting is good for this). Now is time for some Forest Dipping (*see also* page 194) or simply instruct participants to find a spot they like, sit quietly for 10 minutes, decelerate and take in their surroundings, nature, the weather, the view, etc.

Walk: Walk on in pairs for 30–40 minutes. During this section ask everyone to find and collect three small (3–10cm) stones.

Viewpoint: Stop somewhere with a view. Invite anyone in the group who wishes to do so to share the statement they wrote in their notebook at the beginning of the day with the team. Encourage others and offer only positive feedback to these. Next, ask each participant to write the following mission statement formula in their notebooks, '*We will accomplish* _____*by*_____*because of* _____.' This formula for exploring mission statements is taken from Donald Miller's excellent book, *Business Made Simple*[*]. An example he gives for a florist is, 'We bring joy to people by providing the best flowers in the

---

[*]Miller, D. 2021. *Business Made Simple*. HarperCollins.

Houston area because people come alive when they are given flowers by somebody they love.'

Don't fill in the blanks yet but run the Three Stones Make a Wall activity (*see also* page 202) by asking everyone to write one word on each of their stones that they think is relevant to each blank. Three key words from the example above might be 'joy', 'Houston' and 'love'. Pocket these and set off walking again, this time in different pairings.

Walk: Walk on in these new pairs for a further 30–45minutes.

What3Words: Stop somewhere with some space to spread out and ask everyone to choose a spot. Using the What3Words app, issue each person with their three words, e.g. snowballs .vanish.fruit (happens to be one of my favourite places). With these three words and the three words each of you have written on your stones, spend 15 minutes attempting to write a mission statement incorporating all of the six words. It doesn't matter at this stage if they are a bit nonsensical, split into a few sentences or even obviously related to your business as the key is to simply engage and exercise your Outside Thinking, which should be fired up by now. Come back together and share all or some of your work and discuss.

Walk: Walk on again for another 30–45 minutes or until you're 15–30 minutes from the end of the walk.

Throw it away: Stop and do the following two things. Pool all of your stones and discuss, rank and whittle this down to just three between you, the ones you think most important. Using these, ask everyone to revisit the outline mission statement in their notebooks and spend 15 minutes completing this, using these final three key words. They can of course still incorporate their own original words too but have to use the final three.

Walk: Walk back to the starting point. When home, ask everyone to share the contents of their notebooks, their mission statements, even those rejected and their What3Words creations. A good way to do this is via online services like www .miro.com.

Three days later: Schedule a meeting for everyone to attend, where this shared content is reviewed and you work together to review, improve your mission statement or to write and finalize a new one.

The Never'Bored Meeting

First things first, board meetings are inevitable and board meetings are important. But board meetings should not waste time going over figures, KPIs and numbers that everyone in the meeting has had in their possession for up to a week before. The board meeting should only be about pain points and highlights of these, questions raised by these and should be a chance for the founders and executives to gain valuable advice, insights and ideas from the rest of the board.

As we've discovered and explored in chapter 3, the boardroom is no place to have such open, creative discussions. Here is a simple structure for a two-hour (including breaks and bit of housekeeping) meeting, which embeds some outside thinking into discussions:

1) **Pre-prepare**: Ask the board members to supply two days prior to the meeting a maximum of three observations, comments or questions they feel important from the board pack.

2) **Rapid review:** At the meeting, run a short sharp, 10-minute housekeeping and numbers session in your meeting room. Finish by simply listing the board members' feedback and questions.

3) **Load up:** Over the next five minutes present the key questions (three maximum) that you as the founder or executive team would like to address at this meeting. Don't ask for feedback or discuss them yet. If you want, you can incorporate the Three Stones Make a Wall exercise here (*see also* page 202), ready for your walk.

4) **Walk on:** Plan and go for a 30- to 45-minute walk together. Walk, think and talk about these three questions for 10–15 minutes each. For each topic, ensure the pairs change.

5) **Unload:** Return to the meeting room and firstly, pull up your list of key questions and discuss feedback from the walk (allow 30 minutes for this).

6) **Reload:** Finally, bring back up the board members' feedback and questions. Review if they are answered, need answering,

or can be parked until the next meeting (allow 10 minutes for this).

I guarantee your board meetings will be more enjoyable, but more importantly, you'll actually generate and discuss some real, new ideas and solutions.

The Two-Day De-Conference

A half-day or one day of Outside Thinking is good, but two is just better. With more time at your disposal, you and your team can properly decelerate, get your minds deeply into default mode and begin to unlock and free your imaginations fully.

This structure is relatively open to enable you to integrate some of the methods or meeting structures I've already outlined and for you to combine with potential venues and accommodation that you want to use. Ideally, your venue would be an off-grid 'wilderness' camp of some kind and there are plenty out there who can help facilitate this type of event for you to include campfire cooking, entertainment and more, but I fully appreciate that you might want some indoor comfort at the end of a day and somewhere to do some perhaps more formal 'work'. There will be some logistics involved in this activity, mostly around having overnight bags sent on the venue, so participants don't need to carry much at all.

The absolute fixed part of this two-day trip is to arrive and leave on foot, to walk in to the de-conference and to walk out again. These walks need to be approximately three hours and ideally involve a point-to-point journey through some different landscapes:

- Up and over an open hilltop;
- Following a river;
- From inland to the sea.

If you can't organize this, then a circular walk to/from the venue is OK, but try to pick somewhere that offers some of the varied landscapes I covered earlier so that you're not walking the whole time through a deep wood or along a windswept ridge. Even walking from your office, out of the city to the venue can be really effective.

Day One

The first walk is simply about decelerating, talking side-by-side, letting any banter ebb away and doesn't need a lot of structure:

1) Meet and park early-ish (the exact time is really dependent on the time of year; 7 a.m. in summer is OK, but perhaps too dark in November, when 9 a.m. might be better).

2) Present the key aim and objective for the de-conference to the group. For a newly formed team, this could be a straightforward getting-to-know-each-other exercise – it might be a sales kick-off session, an executive or

board event or centred on innovation. Keep this simple and just put the aims into people's heads, no need to discuss.

3) Set out on your three-hour walk, stopping to take in views or landscapes. Don't rush, but try to ensure participants mix up who they are walking and talking with along the way.

4) Arrive at your venue and run your normal conference agenda or integrate in some of the structure from the Outside Strategy Day or Never'Bored Meeting, as required (*see also* pages 220 and 226).

5) End your day with a social event of your choice.

Day Two

Having decelerated, discussed, worked and relaxed on Day One, today is a bit of a flip with one difference to kick off:

1) Kick off the day with a Forest Dipping session (*see also* page 194).

2) Run your normal conference agenda or integrate in some of the structure from the Outside Strategy Day or Never'Bored Meeting, as required (*see also* pages 220 and 226).

3) Now it's time to walk out of the de-conference. This three-hour walk can be an exact re-tracing of your walk in and there are good, metaphorical advantages to doing this. You may be taking the same route, but in reverse your perspective

is shifted and altered. This can be especially powerful if you started your route from your offices. That said, an alternative route through a different landscape has plenty of benefits too, so go for whichever suits your group and/or your location and environment.

4) This walk should be more mentally active and use some Outside Thinking techniques. You can pick and choose a couple of them or a good and simple plan is to use the On a Mission of 3 structure outlined earlier (*see also* page 223). This doesn't have to be specifically about your mission statement and can be drawn from the outcomes and actions of the formal sessions instead.

The Three-Day Retreat and Rethink

Remembering the work of Ruth Atchley and colleagues proving the enormous cognitive benefits of spending four days in nature, Mike Easter's experiences and Rachel Hopman's 20:5:3 rule (*see also* page 150), it should now be firmly fixed in your mind that the creative thinking benefits of a three-day retreat in nature really are transformational. There are only two hard and fast rules for doing this:

1) No technology (except for emergencies and photography). The easiest way to do this is simply to go somewhere off-grid – job done! If you really can't do this for three days, assign a set time every day to check

and respond to messages – ideally at dusk after your day's activities and before the evening social time. Be strict about this.

2) This shouldn't be a major challenge, an extreme event or any kind of team white water rafting experience. It's about being in nature, walking, talking and exploring your Outside Thinking deeply.

Beyond that, the natural world is at your disposal. Find an organizer, facilitator, existing trip and book on it. Go solo, as a team or join a group. Try to do it in landscapes you are naturally drawn to or places that are very different to where you work and live. Embrace the opportunity to do it in different countries or cultural settings and, if you're up for it, slightly out of your comfort zone – including wild camping, for example or staying in a remote refuge.

Accept that this is work, deep work, and not a holiday. Carry questions with you, try some of my methods or exercises or simply walk every day, point-to-point or from a fixed base.

Allow and fund your teams and employees to do this and report back on their experiences. Plan and budget to do so once a year. Allocate funds from your companies' training and development budgets. Scrap plans for your traditional conference and do this instead. The rewards in terms of clear-sighted, creative thinking, of freeing your imaginations and developing radical innovation are multitude.

If you are organizing your own team trip, then here is a simple outline structure to frame your three-day retreat and rethink journey:

Day 1: Just walk, that's about it. Carry a question, decelerate, walk side-by-side and talk.

Day 2: More walking and build in at least three exercises, e.g. Forest Dipping, Natural Storytelling and The Nine-Point Problem (*see also* page 211). Or use On a Mission of 3 (page 223) as a structure.

Day 3: More walking, of course – and Release Your Natural Child, try sharing your Wild Ideas or The Innovation Game (*see also* pages 198 and 205).

A Walkabout

Do you want your venture to be truly radical? Then as a final step towards embracing Outside Thinking, give your staff the freedom to go Walkabout. During a serendipitous meeting at Marrakech airport in 2019 I was chatting to the head of a large and fast-growing tech development and innovation company. The founder allowed and funded all his developers to have one week per year to go on a journey somewhere. It wasn't specifically about walking or nature, but he did insist that they have some sort of adventure, i.e. they weren't funded to lie on a beach or staycation at home. Also, it wasn't part of their holiday allowance. Some skied, some went on cultural trips, others on walking and adventure trips.

The founder was evangelical about the well-being benefits this brought his staff, but more so about the ideas that they always came back with – new ideas for projects they were working on, fresh insights into their work and real, solid ideas for new products and innovations. He had no doubt at all as to the return on investment his firm got from this.

Could you do this? Funnel training budgets into this, allow staff to choose and join an active trip, to set out with some questions, to decelerate, gain wisdom and release their Outside Thinking? I hope some of you can as I truly believe you'll begin to develop some radical innovation as a result.

Thanks to ...

... my late mum and dad for sticking to camping holidays throughout my childhood and through this, introducing me to the best of the British countryside.

... Mr. Kemplay and the school Mountaineering Club for getting me up my first proper peak.

... my early career colleagues at Future Publishing and Microwarehouse for ensuring work was always fun.

... Ben Philips for joining me on my first entrepreneurial journey.

... all the archaeologists I've shared a trench with and made up stories with about the past.

... all of the staff of Teachit for making it such a special and successful entrepreneurial journey.

... the founders of the 180 or so early-stage companies I worked with through the University of Bath.

... Carol Foster for asking me to organize Richard's 50th to Morocco.

... Glenn Smith, Richard Splisbury, Jez Williams, Jim Morrison and Jim Godfrey, who volunteered to be guinea pigs for the first official Outside Thinking walk and offered fantastic feedback.

… Ed Van Rooyen for being my first paying client for Walking Leaders.

… Al Kennedy for being my walking, talking and thinking soulmate.

… the rest of the Outside Thinking community for coming on walking and talking trips every couple of weeks.

… Matt James, Ian Hallsworth, Allie Collins and the team at Bloomsbury.

… Lee Mears for taking time to read my draft and write the foreword.

… everyone who contributed their experiences, research, words or thoughts to this book.

… my three kids, Annie, Isaac and Orla, for camping, walking, talking and exploring with me.

… Siobhain, my wife, my best friend, love of my life, long-term walking and travelling buddy, business partner, encourager, editor, dancing partner, critic and inspiration.

Walk and Talk with Garry

I'm an entrepreneur, business mentor and qualified group walking leader. Walking has always been a key part of my life – whether a simple dog walk, the work commute or preparing for important meetings, outside is where I clear my head, gain perspective and do my best thinking.

I truly believe the best decisions are made with the clarity of mind that comes from a mix of exercise, wildness and engaging with others, and, during my time as a business mentor and advisor, I've found that clients value the opportunity to refocus in the outdoor world.

This is why I often walk with other founders, teams and companies and talk at conferences and events, and I invite entrepreneurs, business leaders and executive teams to join me on adventures that might just change their business and may well influence other areas of their life.

Gaining perspective is a key part of developing creativity and is more likely to develop when you take a break from the ordinary. You won't find your competitive edge at the bottom of an Excel spreadsheet, however large you project it.

Trips range from the ambitious (a week with your team in the Atlas Mountains of North Africa perhaps), the luxurious (exploring the Tramuntana and eating Michelin-starred food in Mallorca) to the more manageable (a half-day one-to-one in the hills of the UK or perhaps as part of your conference) and are all tailored to suit your needs. First step is for us to chat, me to listen and work out what might work for you.

I really look forward to speaking with you, and maybe walking and working with you.

I really look forward to speaking with you, and maybe walking and working with you, your teams or your company.

Garry
www.garrypratt.co.uk

Index